Eighty-One Aces

of the 4th Fighter Group

Frank Speer

Schiffer Military History
Atglen, PA

Acknowledgments

It would be impossible for me alone to write a book such as this. I have had the help of many others as well as being able to refer to books written by friends of mine who have shared the same experiences as I. I am most grateful for the help of the following:

Don Allen, James Ayers, Donald Blakeslee, Keith Braybrooke, James Doddy, Roy Evans, Jim and Jamie Goodson, Dr. Roy Heidicker, Keith Hoey, Charles Konsler, Tom Lowery, Robert Nelson, Mark Phelps, Steve Pisanos, Anne Kramer-Speer, Eugene Speer, and Bruce Zigler.

The following books have been used as references:

The RAF EAGLE SQUADRONS - Philip D. Caine
ESCORT to BERLIN - Gary L. Fry & Jeffrey L Ethell
TUMULT in the CLOUDS - James Goodson
THE INTERROGATOR - Hanns Scharff
FLYING GREEK - Steve Pisanos
KIDD HOFER The Last of the Screwball Aces - Troy White
1000 DESTROYED - Grover Hall
The DEBDEN WARBIRDS - Frank Speer

In addition, I have researched the three Official Squadron Diaries and existing parts of the Tower Diary.

Book Design by Ian Robertson.

Library of Congress Control Number: 2009934853

Printed in China.
ISBN: 978-0-7643-3374-3

We are interested in hearing from authors with book ideas on related topics.

Published by Schiffer Publishing Ltd.
4880 Lower Valley Road
Atglen, PA 19310
Phone: (610) 593-1777
FAX: (610) 593-2002
E-mail: Info@schifferbooks.com.
Visit our web site at: www.schifferbooks.com
Please write for a free catalog.
This book may be purchased from the publisher.
Please include $5.00 postage.
Try your bookstore first.

In Europe, Schiffer books are distributed by:
Bushwood Books
6 Marksbury Avenue
Kew Gardens
Surrey TW9 4JF
England
Phone: 44 (0) 20 8392-8585
FAX: 44 (0) 20 8392-9876
E-mail: Info@bushwoodbooks.co.uk.

Contents

Preface

Over the course of military history certain organizations have distinguished themselves as elite units. Through their valor, dedication, sacrifice, and distinguished service they have placed themselves in a category of honor and renown above all others. The 300 Spartans at Thermopylae, the Old Guard of Napoleon, the 1st Marine Division at Guadalcanal, and the Abbeville Boys of the *Luftwaffe* were all elite units. The 4th Fighter Group blazed a path across the skies of Europe that fully justifies their membership among the elite units of military history. Along the way, the 4th helped defeat the vaunted *Luftwaffe*, including the Abbeville Boys. This book documents the extraordinary story of the 81 pilots of the 4th Fighter Group who achieved the status of Ace. These men contributed greatly to the total of 1,016 German aircraft destroyed by the 4th. This number exceeds the total of enemy planes destroyed by any American Group or Wing not just in World War II, but in any war, before or since. It is incomprehensible that any comparable American organization will ever match this feat.

Students of the air war in Europe will be familiar with many of the aces portrayed in this book. Ralph "Kidd" Hofer, a wild and undisciplined pilot whose short but spectacular career resembled that of the great Frank Luke, the famous American "balloon buster" in World War 1. Known as "the last of the screwball aces," Hofer could not resist engaging the enemy, regardless of the odds or the orders. Readers will enjoy learning about Don Gentile and John Godfrey, the greatest air combat team of all time. Gentile, known as the "one man Air Force," and Godfrey were each great pilots in their own right, but as a team their unconventional tactics confused their opponents and led to their success. Alternating roles as wingman and leader, as the situation required, allowed them to dictate the air combat tactics. *Reichmarshall* Hermann Göring. head of the *Luftwaffe*, referred to them as the "Debden Gangsters," and offered to swap an entire squadron for their destruction! It was Göring who, upon seeing Mustangs of the 4th Fighter Group escorting bombers over Berlin for the first time, turned to his companion and stated, "The war is over. We lost!" The accomplishments and longevity of the career of Vermont Garrison are the stuff of legend. Garrison flew Spitfires and Hurricanes in the Royal Air Force Eagle Squadrons before transferring to the 4th Fighter Group. He became an ace before being shot down and captured. In the Korean War Garrison commanded the 335 th Fighter Squadron "Chiefs" of the 4 th Fighter Interceptor Wing. Flying the superb F-86 Sabre Jet, Garrison scored ten victories, becoming one of only seven pilots in history to achieve the status of ace in two wars! Colonel Garrison went to war again in Vietnam, flying the F-4C Phantom. Garrison was an active participant and leader in an incredible era of aviation evolution.

Speaking of leaders, included in this story of 81 aces is the incomparable commander of the 4th Fighter Group, Colonel Donald J. M. Blakeslee, the greatest air combat leader of all time. From January to November 1944, a critical time in the air war over Europe, Blakeslee pushed, prodded, motivated, and led the Group to dominate and destroy the *Luftwaffe*. Along the way it is conservatively estimated he chalked up over 1200 hours in combat. Blakeslee was instrumental in having his Group convert from the P-47 Thunderbolt to the P-51 Mustang, whose increased range allowed them to escort the bombers to any target and back. His leadership was so respected that he was called upon to lead other new groups into battle.

Frank Speer is uniquely qualified to write a book about the 81 aces of the 4th Fighter Group in World War II. 1st Lieutenant Speer not only served in the Group, he is also one of the aces that he writes about. He served under Colonel Blakeslee, so he knows first hand the quality of his leadership. Speer flew wingman to Kidd Hofer. On 29 May 1944 Lieutenant Speer was shot down by ground fire while strafing a *Luftwaffe* airdrome. Most of the great aces of the Eighth Air Force who were shot down were downed by ground fire during strafing runs, and not by German pilots in air combat. Speer was quite surprised to learn his German captors were well acquainted with the men of the 4th Fighter Group, Colonel Don Blakeslee in particular. In the Korean War the 4th Fighter Interceptor Wing, following up on the accomplishments of the 4th in Worid War II, shot down more enemy MiGs than the entire rest of the United States Air Force combined! Today the men and women of the 4th Fighter Wing continue to be the tip of the spear fighting the enemies of our nation. This marvelous book contributes to the legacy of one of the greatest fighter wings of all time. Frank Speer, ace, warrior, author, and great American patriot, labored long and hard to tell this amazing story of his comrades and fellow 4th Fighter Group aces.

Dr. Roy W. Heidicker
4th Fighter Wing Historian
Seymour Johnson Air Force Base, North Carolina

Foreword

by Mark Phelps

Several years ago I was flying with Frank Speer in my small, two-seat airplane over the farmland and rolling hills of eastern Pennsylvania. I asked him if he'd like to take the controls for a while. I knew Frank hadn't flown an airplane of any kind for decades, but he said, "Sure," swallowed a bit hard before looking around the sky, and then smoothly assumed the feel of the control wheel and rudder pedals. "What heading and altitude do you want?" he asked. I gave him an answer right away, as if I knew exactly what I was doing. But the question had taken me a little by surprise. Under my stewardship the little sportplane had been ambling along in the general direction of our destination within a few hundred feet of whatever altitude it seemed to want to fly at. Below 3,000 feet this is permissible under Federal Aviation Regulations, but not okay for a former fighter pilot, an ace, like Frank. Within seconds the needles were glued on the numbers I had given him; but more importantly, I noticed that Frank's head and eyeballs were twisting and swiveling in all directions. His practiced scan took in the entire sky above, below, ahead, and behind us. For a combat pilot in World War II, keen eyes were as much a weapon as the guns in the wings. The one who saw the enemy first became the hunter; and often, the hunted never saw his adversary until it was too late. Thanks to Frank's ingrained training and instincts, I rested assured that no marauding Messerschmitts would get the better of us this day.

Frank came of age at a time when all young men were thrust into compelling decisions, not about which Wall Street job would bring the highest annual bonus, but rather, which of the military services would be the best way to spend "their war"—and quite possibly expend their very lives. Those who hesitated had their choice made for them by the local draft board. My father-in-law, Elliott Becker, once told me that he chose to enlist in the Navy because he decided that losing his life at sea, should his number come up, would be "a clean death." He reached this decision after talking at length about the subject with his buddies on a street corner in Brooklyn where he grew up. I still find it hard to imagine teenagers standing around talking about how they might face death, but that's the way life was in 1942. Before he died, Elliott also shared with me that he lived every day of his adult life as if it were a gift, because too many of his friends from that street corner never got to come home.

Based largely on Hollywood's image of fighter pilots from World War I, a youthful Frank Speer chose the Army Air Forces (the U.S. Air Force was not established as a separate service until after the war). His aptitude and skills placed him on track for one of the most coveted roles in World War II—flying single-seat fighters. They were the matinee idols of the military—chests chock-a-block with medals and prideful articles written about them in the hometown papers. The men you'll read about in this book are among them. Frank distinguished himself in his training, finishing at or near the top of his class in most categories. Besides the fact that I trust him, I am confident this is so because he was posted to the 4th Fighter Group in England—and I have been studying the Fourth for decades. Its pilots accounted for more enemy aircraft destroyed than any other Allied unit during the war. They personified the best of the best.

Part of the reason was the core contingent of 4th Group pilots got their start in the British RAF, many as members of the three Eagle Squadrons. The Eagles were Americans who volunteered for flying duty long before Pearl Harbor, and jeopardized their citizenship by violating our neutrality laws and going to the aid of England in her time of most dire need. As often as not, their reasons for leaving home had more to do with seeking adventure in the skies than lofty political principles. But they came to respect the British passionately, and to despise the German enemy with equal intensity.

The three Eagle Squadrons were rewarded by the British Royal Air Force with a posting to one of the RAF's pre-war permanent bases. Debden was located about 20 miles south of Cambridge, and it consisted of brick buildings with steam heat. Enlisted "batmen" served as a sort of butler for each officer, shining shoes, taking care of laundry, and even gently waking them for a dawn mission, sometimes after a late night of youthful horseplay. After the Eagles were incorporated into the USAAF in October 1942, Debden became famous for its dances and other social events. It wasn't unusual to see combat aircraft of all types parked overnight near the control tower for one of Debden's soirees. They were flown there by an assortment of the USAAF's high-ranking officers from air bases all over England.

Frank joined the Fourth Group not as one of the original renegade volunteers, but rather as a replacement pilot who worked his way through the U.S. military, following the rules. And by performing at the highest level. And so, he found himself among the most experienced—and some say the most eccentric—band of brothers to take to the skies above Europe. Someday, people will look back on these men in the way we now remember the storied Knights of the Round Table. Much of their humanness will be forgotten. What will remain is the legend, stretched to unbelievability, yet grounded in actual historical fact.

I've been privileged to meet and know Frank and several other pilots of the 4th Group whom you will read about within these pages. To me they are the stuff of story books, because the histories I read about them as a child were like story books to me. But as I met and got to know them, their human qualities and faults shone through, which, to me, made their heroics that much more... well, heroic. I once asked Herb Blanchfield what it felt like to jump from an airplane that was crippled by enemy fire. His response was matter-of-fact, and it helped me to understand. He simply shrugged his shoulders and said that you just have to do what you have to do. He lightly joked about the unappealing alternative. As incredible as it seems to me to this day, it truly was not extraordinary to them. Seeing Herb's shoulders shrug, taking in the nonchalant grin on his face as he responded to my question, I was able to appreciate that, to him, jumping out of burning airplanes was just part of their lives at the time. And as such, was "No big deal."

But, of course, it was a big deal. As big a deal as there ever was in history. It was a time when thousands of high powered, wickedly silver Mustangs roamed the heavens above Europe, seeking out their opponents, who were equally well-equipped for battle to the death. We understand a lot more about the pilots of the Fourth thanks to a memoir written about them by the Group Public Relations officer, Grover Hall. A second-generation newspaperman from Mobile, Alabama, Hall was able to capture much of the essence of his pilots—their humanness. The book is titled *1000 Destroyed*. Though it's long since out of print, you can find copies on the internet.

As part of his own passion for preserving the Fourth's legacy, Frank Speer has written three previous books about his experiences flying with the Group. This latest effort is his best attempt at chronicling as much as he can on all 81 aces who flew in their ranks. For some there wasn't much to find. For others, however, you'll read material not found anywhere else in print. And most important, what you'll be reading here are the stories told by one who walked the flight line and ate in the officers' mess with these men at their base in Debden, England, and flew with them into harm's way on a daily basis. There can be no closer association than to have shared combat.

As one born seven years after the end of World War II, it has been fascinating for me to read these and other accounts of the pilots' heroism, and also the follow-up on the ones who survived. Like Frank, they blended back into the fabric of American life, sort of. In fact, they could never be the same again. And yet, they assumed the roles of normal men, as if the war had never happened. And we who lived among them never knew, unless we asked. Even then we could never know the whole story.

When I was growing up in the 1950s we had a delivery driver named Everett Soule who brought bread to our house every week (remember that?). I remember his name, I'm sure, because it was painted on the side of his truck. What I also remember about Everett Soule is that he had two fingers missing from one of his hands. Of course, I never asked.

Maybe they were blown off by shrapnel on Iwo Jima, or shot off by a German machine gunner on Omaha Beach. Or maybe he lost them to frostbite in Bastogne during the Battle of the Bulge. Of course, it's entirely possible he lost his fingers to a power saw in his basement. Now, I doubt I'll ever know.

But I remember Everett Soule. I remember that he was a part of my very ordinary life. Yet it is readily possible, even likely, that he was also part of something so extraordinary that it defies understanding to all but those who were there. And when they're gone, vital elements of their history will die with them. The men you will read about in these pages are the same way. Some never had the chance to return to their normal lives here in the States. They will remain kids for eternity; forever young. Those who did come home were changed, like my father-in-law, also forever. But in every case, these men were part of legendary times, the likes of which will never be seen again. The pilots of the Fourth wrote history in the skies above Europe; but large parts of their stories will be lost to future generations, as fleeting as the wispy condensation trails that traced their paths at 30,000 feet more than six decades ago. But with Frank's book, you can read about their exploits from someone who was there—one of them; one of the aces of the Fourth Fighter Group.

Frank, I salute you and your brethren. And I thank God you were there when we needed you.

Cheers,
Mark Phelps

Introduction

Since recorded history men have engaged in duels to the death. Early records tell of the gladiators in the Colosseum having at each other until one is defeated or dead, with the victim, if still alive, having his fate finally decided by the vertical position of the Emperor's thumb. Gladiators who lived long enough to become frequent victors were considered heroes, and were afforded many advantages.

Decades later men known as knights, generally on horseback, became the gladiators of their time. Mostly the victors' strategy was to unhorse his opponent and hack him up with his choice of weapon unless the victim yielded. The most successful of these also were considered heroes and were afforded many rewards.

In later centuries, with the advent of the airplane, jousts in the air slowly evolved into a match between a different type of gladiator or knight. In World War I, the airplane was originally used for reconnaissance of enemy positions in order better to conduct offenses. The plane, with its enhanced range, had more capability to observe enemy movements than the tethered balloons formerly used for this purpose. Both sides in WWI used this new weapon for the same purpose until such time as opposing forces decided to claim territorial rights over certain sectors of the sky. Early attempts to secure these individual territories began with a primitive warfare where the combatants threw rocks, or shot pistols or rifles at each other and became generally obnoxious.

Various improvements in armament led to observers in the back seat being armed with movable machine guns that could only generate angled or deflection shots at enemy aircraft. Soon forward firing machine guns were installed, creating considerably enhanced firing possibilities. Now the pilot was able to maneuver his plane into a favorable position before he himself fired the guns. This configuration opened up a whole new opportunity for both offensive and defensive tactics and began an era of one-on-one aerial combat.

The victors in these combats were determined with little chance of mistake when the vanquished went down in flames or his plane disintegrated in air with no parachute to delay his fall. Planes were improved, engines became more powerful, and machine guns became more trustworthy. Soon there were men who became more successful than their peers in downing enemy planes, and recognition of their victories became a matter of record. Somewhere in the evolution of this method of combat the title "Ace" was bestowed on any pilot who downed five enemy planes. It did not matter that a rear-seat observer may have done the shooting, the pilot got the credit.

As World War II began, the fighter plane, in the European Theatre, became a one seat vehicle with far advanced designs and only forward firing guns. In addition, cameras were installed to record the effectiveness of the machine guns as they were being fired. It was then no longer necessary to have a witness to the destruction of an enemy plane. The camera never lied, except when it was inoperative, or the lens was fogged up, or destruction happened after the guns were no longer firing. It was usually, however, a reliable source of information.

Pilots were well trained and knowledgeable in both offensive and defensive tactics. With the advent of long range fighters, such as the P-38, P-47, and the P-51 in the European Theatre, the combat extended far into German territory, and the *Luftwaffe* became very aggressive in defending their "homeland." This resulted in many aerial combats as the Allies persistently attacked the Nazi infrastructure. The aerial battles that ensued saw many German as well as Allied fighters destroyed as the Allies tried to protect their bombers over enemy territory. These combats saw many pilots become aces as aerial victories accumulated.

Eventually the *Luftwaffe* tactics changed, with the German fighters reluctant to face such destructive forces unnecessarily. They chose to save their fighters for selected attacks on the bombers, avoiding the Allied fighters as much as possible. In turn, the Allies began to attack the Germans on their airfields. This program was extremely successful in destroying enemy aircraft, but it was bought at a dreadful cost of Allied planes destroyed and pilots lost to the walls of flak and small arms fire directed at them as they swooped low over the airfields. Attacking German airdromes was a veritable hell into which those fighters roared so low that their propellers churned up dust; the preferred method of attack. Most fighters would much rather fight in the air rather than strafe airdromes; they felt they had much more chance of being victorious. A fact of life in this battle was that many more of our pilots ended up as Prisoners of War as the result of strafing airdromes than as the result of aerial combat. Of our 81 aces in the 4th Fighter Group, responsible for nearly 600 kills, roughly 46% of their victories were accomplished by strafing, while 22% became POWs and 18% were KIA (Killed in Action).

So what constitutes being an ace? Elitists from the beginning have required five aerial kills, even though the pilot may not have been the shooter. They have maintained that stance to this day. The Army Air Corps, however, wrote orders designating pilots as an "ace" without regard to the location of an enemy plane destroyed. A copy of one such order follows. The decision will not go away without controversy, since many modern fighter planes now carry two pilots, one flying the plane and the other, a weapons specialist, doing the actual release of armament. Advancements in weapons have already led to fighters with stealth capabilities, unseen by the enemy, and not seeing the enemy except by radar, shooting him down miles away. Does this type of victory lead to a pilot becoming an ace? And, which one?

The conclusion I draw, for the purposes of this book, is that an ace is anyone who has destroyed five enemy planes whether on the ground or in the air! I'm sure the bomber crews cared little where the destruction took place as long as the enemy was no longer able to return to the fray.

This book recognizes 81 Aces of the 4th Fighter Group and their part in the destruction of over 1,000 *Luftwaffe* planes during WWII.

I

Eagle Squadrons

Prior to the United States' entry into WWII many Americans volunteered for service in the RCAF and the RAF. The RAF had sustained many losses of pilots in the Battle of Britain and had consequently called for volunteers to replace their diminished ranks. An organization called the Knight Committee began recruiting volunteers with flying experience and was responsible for recruiting 90% of the members of the Eagle Squadrons primarily from the ranks of civilian pilots in the United States. Thousands volunteered; many who were ineligible for the U.S. Army Aviation Cadet program, those who sought adventure, and some who felt it was a patriotic duty. 244 American pilots were accepted and were to fly with the Eagle Squadrons.

Most trained in the RCAF in Canada and some in the States. Their training completed, the next step was an OTU (operational training unit) in England. There they learned to fly Miles Masters trainers, Hurricanes, and Spitfires prior to assignment to a squadron. Once assigned, they were indoctrinated into formation flying and current tactical maneuvers under the guidance of English squadron and flight commanders. OTU completed, they became active in combat missions; convoy escort, bomber escorts, and strafing.

Once the United States entered the war, the Eagle Squadrons were invited to become a part of the United States Army Air Corps. Much negotiation ensued in order to accomplish this program in an orderly fashion. Organization of the group entity, rank of the participants, and compensation to the British for both training and the Spitfires to be transferred had to be considered. Initially, the group needed Spitfires since there were no American fighter planes available, and of course, trained crews were needed to keep them operational.

Once these problems were resolved, the pilots were given U.S. pilot wings and the Fourth Fighter Group became operational on 29 September 1942.

A copy of a calendar which hung in one of the pilots' " Ready Rooms" bearing signatures of original Eagle Squadron members listed below.

Signatures

71 Squadron
Col, Chesley Pererson
Capt. Oscar Coen
Lt. T. Andrews
Lt. W. O'Regan
Lt. James dark Jr.
Lt. G. Ross
Lt. A. Hopson
Lt R. Priser
Lt Howard Hively
Lt. Henry Mills
Lt Duane Beeson
Lt. R. Care
Lt. Steve Pisanos
Lt. Eugene Peters
Lt Vemon Boehle
Lt. Jim Du Forsy

121 Squadron
Col. Donald Blakeslee
Capt. Sheldon Edner
Lt Gilbert Halsey
Lt. Frank Boyles
Lt. E. Beattie
Lt. P.O. Smith
Lt. A. D. Young
Lt. J. M. Osbome
Lt C. V. Padgett
Lt. Frank Fink
Lt R. G. Patterson
Lt. K. G. Smith
Lt. George Carpenter
Lt. Paul Ellington
Lt. L. M. Bianding
Lt. J. R. Happel
Lt. Roy Evans
Lt. Aubrey Stanhope
Lt. E. Booth

133 Squadron
Lt. Don Gentile
Lt. Leroy Gover
Lt. Carl Miley
Lt. Don Nee
Lt. G. Smart
Lt. H. Ayres
Lt. Joe Bennett
Lt. Mike Sobanski
Lt. James Goodson
Lt. L. Riley
Lt. Erwin Keller
Lt. Robert Messinger
Lt. Pete Pibus

II

The 4th Fighter Group

The 4th Fighter Group was activated 12 September 1942. Based in Debden, England, it was made up of the three Eagle Squadrons of the Royal Air Force (No.71, No.121, and No.133). As they were transferred from the Royal Air Force to the United States Army Air Force, in the Eighth Air Force they became designated as the 334th, 335th, and 336th Squadrons.

They flew their first combat mission under American colors on 2 October 1942, still flying British Spitfires. Upon receipt of an adequate number of P-47 Thunderbolts and crews skilled in their maintenance, the Group converted to P-47s in March 1943. In February 1944 the group switched to P-51 Mustangs, which they continued to fly until the end of the war in Europe. They flew their last combat mission on 25 April 1945. They had become the top scoring Allied Fighter Group in the war, having destroyed 1016 enemy aircraft for a loss of 241 of their own planes.

It is of note that their losses were disproportionately high due to the fact that their combat was always over enemy territory and many of their losses were suffered as the result of flak (anti-aircraft fire).

They were the first fighter group to penetrate German air space.
They were selected to escort bombers on the first shuttle bombing run to land in Russia.
They were the first to escort bombers over Berlin.
They were awarded a Unit Citation for destroying 189 enemy aircraft for the period 5 March to 24 April 1944.

III

Headquarters Squadron

The Headquarters Squadron was made up of true leaders. Most had flown Hurricanes, Spitfires, Thunderbolts, and Mustangs.

Some had flown in the RCAF, the RAF, and the USAAF, while others had flown in the Pacific Theater in P-40s and P-38s.

They were not necessarily high scoring, but attentive to their duties of melding the three squadrons into a group with a high degree of readiness and esprit-de-corps.

Colonel Donald J. M. Blakeslee
Colonel James A. Clark Jr.
Lt. Colonel Seldon R. Edner
Lt. Colonel Claiborne H. Kinnard
Captain Shelton W. Monroe
Lt. Colonel Jack Oberhansly
Colonel Chesley G. Peterson
Colonel Everett W. Stewart
Lt. Colonel Sidney S. Woods

FRANK - I'd like to put a squadron crest here, but the mock-up you had showed the Eaqgle Squadron crests, so if you have another Headquarters Squadron crest I'll put it here.

Colonel **DONALD J. M. BLAKESLEE**

Colonel Donald Blakeslee, from Fairport Harbor, Ohio, was a fighter pilot's fighter pilot. He was considered by many to be the greatest fighter pilot of WWII. Respected by his men, his superiors, and the *Luftwaffe*, he spurred his 4th Fighter Group to become the top-scoring Allied fighter group of the war. Colonel Jim Clark, his Group Operations Officer, said of Don, "He always knew what to do in combat, never got lost, and always got us back home."

Before the war Don lived and worked in Detroit, Michigan. Disaster struck when he loaned his Waco airplane to a friend who cracked it up. Don had no insurance, but still had a craving to fly. He heard of a Royal Canadian Air Force office in Windsor, Canada, so, armed with his logbook, he applied for training and was accepted. He felt no real animosity toward the Germans nor zeal to fight them, but he wanted to fly high-speed planes and to be where the action was. Eventually his feelings changed and he grew to hate the Nazis, particularly the yellow-nosed "Abbeville Boys," a crack *Luftwaffe* group. This attitude drove him to be relentless in combat. He went through the RCAF training program, but insisted on going into the British Royal Air Force rather than staying as an instructor in the RCAF.

Training completed, he requested a short leave to say goodbye to his family, which his Canadian superiors were reluctant to grant because they had no hold on their U.S.-citizen trainees. Some had graduated from their flight training and gone home never to return. The officers finally relented, and after a short leave Don returned, eager to get into the fray. The American volunteers were assigned to three "Eagle Squadrons." Don served in each of the three, eventually becoming CO of the 133rd.

He transferred into the U.S. 4th Fighter Group as a major, when it was commissioned, and became its Group Executive Operations Officer in May 1943. In January 1944 he became the Commanding Officer. There he began to build his group's reputation, as time after time he succeeded in initiating innovative methods of destroying the *Luftwaffe* as the 4th protected U.S. bombers on their offensive forays over the Nazi-controlled Continent. He was a great leader and inspired confidence in his men, whose aggressiveness mirrored his intensity and culminated in the production of 81 Aces in the group by the end of hostilities on VE Day.

Blakeslee's priority was clear: he would make the 4th the most productive Allied fighter unit in Europe. He was critical of the RAF formation of four planes lined astern. This placed the best pilot as leader and the least experienced as "Tail-end Charlie," which made

the newest pilots most vulnerable in combat. Blakeslee changed to a more line-abreast style with two flights of two, each able to support one another in a fight. On the 15 April 1943 he claimed the first German fighter to be shot down by a P-47. Like many ex-Eagles, Don was skeptical of the huge American fighter after many combat hours flying the nimble British Spitfire. He dove his Thunderbolt from 23,000 feet to 500 feet, following and shooting down a Focke Wulf-190, showing that the P-47 could out-dive the 190. He later remarked "By God it ought to dive, it certainly won't climb."

The P-47s were fairly successful throughout the year, but in February 1944, due to Blakeslee's insistence, the P-47s were replaced with the longer-range P-51s, with his assurance that he would have them operational within a day of the changeover. This he accomplished, despite his pilots having an average of only 40 minutes in the 51s prior to their first combat flight.

On 28 February the first P-51 mission for the 4th was flown to Noball, near Paris. On 4 March Blakeslee led the first escort mission to Berlin. During March and April the 4th destroyed 370 enemy aircraft. In fact, on the fifth day of April the 4th destroyed 45 in aerial combat and ground strafing, and on the 8th destroyed 33 more in aerial combat. This achievement did not go unnoticed by the Nazis, and in May, Berlin radio broadcast a message, "You North American gangsters in red-nosed Mustangs will be prosecuted in People's Court as war criminals!" On 11 April General Eisenhower personally decorated Col. Blakeslee and Capt. Don Gentile with the Distinguished Service Cross. This took place just two days before Gentile's unfortunate accident, where he pranged his plane *Shangri La* as he made a low pass in front of

a group of correspondents gathered to record his return from his last combat flight prior to going home to the States on leave. He was being celebrated for having destroyed 30 enemy planes during his first combat tour. Happily he survived, but his error did not sit well with Don Blakeslee:

"On 17 April 1944 six of us bright eyed and bushy tailed newly trained recruits arrived at Debden, having completed our Operational Training Unit schooling at Goxhill, England. Most of our day was spent routinely checking into the various operational entities. There is no question that we were somewhat apprehensive of our final interview that evening. We were to meet with the Group Commander, Colonel Don Blakeslee. We assembled in his office to wait for him. He made an imposing entrance, dressed in his leather A-2 jacket and his 40-mission crush hat. He looked like he had just returned from a mission.

He explained, rather briskly, the routines we were to follow and how we were expected to fit into the Group. Warming to his subject, he stated that we had just arrived from the States, where we had a myriad of rules and regulations governing our conduct in the air. Now he expected us to forget them, and that every time we flew at Debden we were not to return to base and land without having broken all of those rules. He continued by telling us that in the 4th there are SOPs (Standard Operating Procedures), and that if you are caught breaking any of them, or if you 'Prang a kite' through pilot error you'll never fly with us again.

He demanded **aggressive pilots**, but there was to be **strict discipline**! He saluted, turned, and left, leaving us with a very lasting impression of what was to be expected of us."

On 29 May the 4th flew a successful escort mission to Poznan, Poland, the longest fighter mission to date. This was preliminary to the anticipated "Shuttle Run" from England to Russia.

On D-Day, 6 June, the 4th flew missions all day protecting the invasion forces on the ground. It was a disastrous day, with the loss of 10 pilots KIA, POW, or MIA, but five replacements arrived to help shore up the roster. On 21 June Blakeslee led 64 Mustangs in support of three combat wings of B-17s on a pioneer shuttle run to Piryatin, Russia. They arrived on course and on time after a seven-hour fifteen minute flight. Subsequently they continued on to Italy and returned to Debden on 5 July.

On 30 October Colonel Blakeslee was grounded, having flown in excess of 500 combat missions and 1000 hours of combat. This action was taken to preclude the possibility of his being shot down to become a POW. This had just happened to Col. Hubert Zemke, the Commander of the 56th Fighter Group (the 4th's friendly rival in the race to become the leader in number of enemy aircraft destroyed).

Although still in command of the 4th, Col. Blakeslee went on a much deserved leave to the States. While there he was married, in spite of his stated philosophy that "fighter pilots and women don't mix." An unfortunate interview where this philosophy was made public prompted a deluge of critical letters from women across the country, causing Don to recant, insisting that he was misquoted.

Blakeslee liked the action of combat and disliked administrative duties, but he put it all together in leading the 4th Fighter Group in the destruction of 1,016 enemy aircraft. By January 1945 his group had destroyed more enemy aircraft than the entire U.S. Air Corps had destroyed in WWI (763). Don himself was credited with 17.5 destroyed, but denied his success was due to being a better shot. He said he was "just a better hunter." His many awards included the Distinguished Service Cross with Oak Leaf Cluster, Silver Star and Bar, U.S. Distinguished Flying Cross with 7 OLC, British Distinguished Flying Cross, and the Air Medal with 3 OLC.

He subsequently served in a number of assignments in the U.S., where his "boring" non-combat administrative duties occasioned him to be somewhat testy with his superior officers.

Don eventually retired in Florida as a Colonel, where he lived and, in true Blakeslee style, jealously guarded his privacy. He was frequently asked to write his memoirs, but always responded, "Aw, someone will catch me in a lie." As an admirer and friend of Don, my recent suggestion that I visit him elicited this response:

"Come on over if you want, but don't expect much from me, because I'll be watching the football game and swearing at the coaches and players, and **Leave your damn tape recorder at home**!"

On 3 September 2008 this great fighter pilot, a man's man, loved by most, hated by some (especially the *Luftwaffe*), but respected by all, left us forever to join his beloved wife.

Colonel **JAMES A. CLARK, Jr.**

James A. Clark hailed from Westbury, Long Island, New York. He was a tall, handsome man, the nephew of Tommy Hitchcock, a celebrated member of the famous Lafayette Escadrille of World War I. Jim left school to join the RAF. He completed the routine training necessary to be a combat pilot with the RAF and was assigned to the 71st Eagle Squadron June 1942. Upon the inception of the 4th Fighter Group that September he was assigned to the

Eagle Squadron members-l-r: Robert Book, James Clark, William O'Regan, Chesley Peterson, Richard McMinn, Stan Anderson, and Oscar Coen.

334th Squadron, where he eventually became CO. In March 1944 he became Group Operations Officer, and in September, as a Lieutenant Colonel, he became acting Group and Station CO in the absence of Donald Blakeslee. Prior to becoming Group Operations Officer he served as Assistant Military Attaché for Air, U.S. Embassy, London.

Clark led many missions. He had the ability to carry the courses, altitudes, weather conditions, and rendezvous times in his head, but was always rather aloof and reserved. As Deputy Commander of the Group he was a perfect match for Donald Blakeslee. Blakeslee was prone to be rough, swore, and frequently lost his temper, while Clark remained quiet and cool. But both had the respect of every man in the Group. They led by example, and every man would follow them unquestioningly.

Clark flew Spitfires, then Thunderbolts, and finally Mustangs. He led the first mission in Mustangs. He believed that, although it was definitely more dangerous to strafe enemy aircraft on the ground than destroy them in the air, it was a more productive way to accomplish the goal of reducing the threat of the *Luftwaffe* before the coming D-day invasion. Accordingly, on March 21, 1944, he led the Group on a tree-level, spread-formation swing through south, central, and northern France strafing airfields, destroying 21 enemy aircraft and damaging planes, trains, and airfields. Though successful, the mission was not without loss, with seven of our planes shot down, two of our pilots killed, four became POWs, and one evaded and returned. For his innovative approach and audacious conduct of this mission Jim was awarded the Silver Star. Many such raids followed, and the toll on the *Luftwaffe* was extensive.

During his tour with the 4th Jim made headlines in the London Evening News when he married Lady Bridget Elliot, daughter of an English Earl.

He was credited with 16 *Luftwaffe* planes destroyed and was awarded the Silver Star, the Distinguished Flying Cross w/OLCs, the Air Medal w/OLCs, and the Distinguished Unit Award.

Upon discharge at the end of the war he spent four years in civilian activities, then returned to the Air Force as Commander of a jet fighter training group. Later, he became president of a company servicing crop dusting planes, president of a gold mining company, and then an executive in an air freight company. He retired in 1980 and died in 1990, survived by his wife, Armeme, a daughter Carey, and a son Christopher.

Lt. Colonel **SELDON R. EDNER**

In 1941 Seldon Edner left his home in San Jose, California, where he had graduated from San Jose State College. He had been found lacking in qualifications for the Army Aviation Cadet program, and with 500 hours of flight time he went to England to join the RAF. He arrived six months after the Battle of Britain. Pilots and planes were in short supply. Volunteers were pressed into combat almost immediately after a short training period. Seldon was assigned to No. 121 Eagle Squadron flying Hurricanes, formed May 1941 and operational in sixty days at Kirton-in-Lindsey. There he flew Spitfires with this group that destroyed hundreds of planes, ships, locos, tanks, and weapon stores. They paid a high price for their aggressiveness, as one of every three was killed.

On a Dieppe raid Seldon shot down one enemy aircraft. His plane was badly damaged, but he nursed it back to England. He downed five more before being transferred as a Major to the 4th Fighter Group, 336th Squadron in September 1942. In December, having shown signs of being a calm and capable leader, he was promoted to Lt. Col. and made CO of the 336th Squadron. In January he was made 4th Fighter Group Operations Officer, and in February he became Executive Officer. He was very active in combat, and in February 1944 he led the Group on seven missions. On 8 March 1944, while leading the Group to Berlin, it is believed he received a flak hit and he was captured to become a POW.

After the war he served in different military capacities. Greece was receiving aid under the Truman Doctrine when in 1947 the Communists in Greece began a civil war against the Greek Government. In 1948 Seldon Edner was sent to Greece as an American Military Observer. In January 1949 the news was reported that Seldon and his Greek pilot had been shot down by Communist guerrillas. Ambassador Henry F. Grady said Edner was making an unarmed observation flight over the Karpenision Battle area when his plane crashed in hilly country. The Yugoslav news protested to the Security Council that the two men were taking part in strafing-bombing missions. (It would seem unusual for strafing-bombing missions to be conducted by an AT-6, which is the type plane Seldon is reported to have been flying.) Amidst this controversy, the only thing certain seems to be that Seldon died doing what he thought was right.

Lt. Colonel **CLAIBORNE H. KINNARD**

Col. Kinnard, already a much decorated fighter pilot, came to the 4th Fighter Group in September 1944 from his former position as Group Commander of the 355th Fighter Group. He was appointed Deputy Group Commander, reporting to Lt. James Clark, acting C.O. during Col. Blakeslee's leave in the States. On 1 Nov. Col. Claiborne assumed command of the 4th. He faced a tough job revitalizing the group. Most of the top-scoring aces were gone, having finished their tours and rotated to the States or having succumbed to enemy action, being killed or becoming POWs.

He became C.O. of a high-spirited but inexperienced group of rookies with little in-depth squadron leadership. To compound the difficulty of restoring the esprit-de-corps of the group, the severe winter weather cut down on necessary flying practice. In addition, the *Luftwaffe* no longer rose to attack with their customary frequency and ferocity; some pilots flew over 100 combat hours without ever seeing a German fighter.

Kinnard led the group on many missions opposed only by flak, but met Germans on only a couple, managing to score six victories in his plane "Man 'O War." The group had lost its sizzle with little hope of change.

On 29 November 1944 he left to become C.O. of another group where he did a creditable job. At the end of the war his record included 25 enemy aircraft destroyed, and he had been awarded the DSC, Silver Star, DFC with 6 OLC, AM with 6 OLC, the *Croix-de-Guerre* with Palm, and the DUC. He passed away in July 1966 of a brain tumor.

Captain **SHELTON W. MONROE**

Captain Monroe was from Waycross, Georgia. He entered the 4th Fighter Group, 334th Squadron January 1944, where he was assigned until January 1945, when he was transferred to 335th Squadron until April 1945. In April he was transferred to the 4th R&R Squadron on detached service ferrying P-51Ds to Sweden, where he acted as an adviser to the Swedish Air Force.

While with the 4th he had been Assistant Squadron Operations and Gunnery Officer and later Group Operations Officer. After his first tour of duty he was on U.S. leave 19 August 1944 to 1 November 1944. He subsequently was killed in action in the Korean War.

In WWII he had 8.8 German planes destroyed and was awarded the Silver Star, the Distinguished Flying Cross with Three Oak Leaf Clusters, and the Air Medal with numerous Oak Leaf Clusters.

Lt. Col. **JACK OBERHANSLY**

Lt. Colonel Jack Oberhansly, from Spanish Fork, Utah, was commissioned and received his wings 12 December 1941 at Luke Field, Phoenix, Arizona. He joined the 14th Pursuit Group, 48th Pursuit Squadron. He transferred to the 78th Fighter Group, 82nd Squadron on 11 May 1942. He became the Commanding Officer of the 82nd Squadron 7 August 1943 to May 1944. He became Deputy Commanding Officer of the78th Fighter Group in August 1944.

He came to the 4th Fighter Group as Deputy Commanding Officer 4 December 1944. The next day he became acting Group Commander. He spent the next three months with the 4th during a period of little activity. Bad weather precluded much flying, and the *Luftwaffe* fighters likewise were not active.

In February, he was transferred to the 372nd Fighter Group as Commanding Officer.

Oberhansly, with 150 combat hours in his plane "Iron Ass" had nine victories and awards of the Distinguished Flying Cross with three Oak Leaf Clusters, the Air Medal with five Oak Leaf Clusters, and the *Croix de Guerre* with Palm.

After the war ended, he served as Commanding Officer of the 191st Fighter Squadron of the Utah Air National Guard from 1946 to 1948. He died 6 September 1981.

Colonel **CHESLEY G. PETERSON**

Chesley Peterson, from Santaquin, Utah, knew as a boy that aviation was his love. It started when a barnstormer sat down an old crate on his father's alfalfa field and asked to use it for landings. His father agreed, with the condition that the pilot take Chesley and his sister for a flight. That sold Pete on flying. Later he went to work as an aircraft inspector for Douglas Aircraft in California. He was like most aspiring fighter pilots, in that he wanted to fly big fast planes. The only way to do this was to enlist in the military service. Turned down by the U.S. Army Air Corps as being underage, he was recruited by Col. Charles Sweeny as part of an organized effort to bring American pilots to the aid of the Allies by way of Canada. But Pete wanted to go into the Royal Air Force rather than the Royal Canadian Air Force.

Getting to England was a difficult feat. He finally got to Canada, from whence he shipped to England. Following delays, he made his way into the RAF, assigned to No.71 Squadron, which was involved in active combat. They had the usual missions until the Dieppe Raid 19 August 1941. On their third sortie for the day, they found a British convoy being attacked by 20 German Ju-88s with fighter escort. Chesley attacked a Ju-88 on its bombing run, forcing it to drop its bombs prematurely, but his Spitfire was severely damaged by the bomber's tail gunner. The bomber crashed into the sea, but Pete was forced to bail out of his burning Spit into the Channel. He was rescued and back in action in a few days.

During his stay in 71 Squadron, he tackled all combat with an aggressiveness that endeared him to the English as well as to his men. He was promoted to Flight Lt., the first American in the Eagle Squadrons to be promoted above the enlisted rank of Pilot Officer. In October he received the Distinguished Flying Cross and in November, upon the accidental death of Squadron Leader Stanley Meares, Peterson became Squadron Leader with the command burden on his shoulders at the age of 21. He was well thought of by the RAF as being very capable and having good leadership qualities instilling strong loyalties among his men.

In December, the announcement that Japan had attacked Pearl Harbor and the U.S. had declared war caused much celebration in the Eagle Squadrons. They felt they now had new allies, the United States. As the U.S. presence grew, transfer of the Eagle Squadrons to the U.S. Army Air Corps became an increasing desire. The U.S. wanted the Eagles, but the RAF did not want to give them up. It became a very slow process with many considerations. The question of rank became a problem, especially in regard to the Sergeant Pilots, since the U.S. had no equivalent rank. Also there was controversy over transferring the squadrons as units versus seeding other squadrons with individual pilots from the Eagles.

Peterson was adamant, in that if they were to plan to break up the squadrons they would not transfer. Finally these differences were resolved. The new U.S. Group would be the 4th Fighter Group, and would consist of three squadrons (334, 335, and 336) based at Debden, a permanent RAF station just south of

THE STARS AND STRIPES — Wednesday, Sept. 8, 1943

They Told 'Pete' He Couldn't Fly

Now, at 23, He's Youngest Fighter Group Chief in ETO, Nine Nazis to His Credit

By Arthur W. White
Stars and Stripes Staff Writer

HQ, — FIGHTER GROUP, England, Sept. 7—Four years ago he washed out of Randolph Field for "lack of flying ability." Today, at 23, Lt. Col. Chesley G. Peterson is the youngest fighter group commander in the Eighth Air Force.

Since he joined the Eagle Squadron of the RAF he has chalked up a score of nine German planes, seven probables and five damaged. And he has maintained a discreet silence about his "lack of flying ability."

"I've never liked to admit it before," he said. "I've always declared that I left because the authorities discovered that I was under age. But, so help me, I was kicked out."

Eager to Push Nazis Back

The tall, blond young airman, whose appointment to lead the old Eagle Squadron is believed to presage his promotion to a full colonelcy, is enthusiastic about fighters. His eagerness for the job in hand was evident at a London press conference Monday, his first since he was named group leader.

He said then that the air offensive six months ago looked like a much bigger job than it turned out to be, and with typical enthusiasm he added:

"We're rapidly pushing back the Luftwaffe front lines toward Germany. We're putting the Luftwaffe in a position where we are going to be top dog over his own territory."

"Pete"—the nickname his men have given him—looks harmless enough when he's taking it easy, stretching out his long legs and sucking his PX briar and making a noise you can hear a mile off. But he likes to fly. And when he's flying

Here is Chesley Peterson when he was only 21 years old but a flight lieutenant in the RAF and commander of the Eagle squadron.

Cambridge. They would still fly Spitfires with mostly RAF ground crews. Wing Commander Raymond Duke Woolley, on loan from the RAF, would be in charge of flying of the Debden Group, and Col. Edward Anderson, a regular U.S. Army Air Corps officer, would be in command. Other considerations were resolved, and all were grateful for the change from RAF pay to the considerably higher rate of the Army Air Corps pay scale. The transfer was completed on 12 September 1942, when the 4th was officially activated. Peterson was made a Major upon transfer. A month later in October he was promoted to Lieutenant Colonel.

The Group flew Spitfires on combat missions until they received P-47 Thunderbolts and trained in them. Then, on 10 March 1943 Peterson led the first operational flight of P-47s to Ostend. On 15 April he led a fighter sweep, known as a Rodeo, to Cassel, where they encountered five FW-190s. Pete shot one down in flames, but blew a cylinder head and headed for home. He had to bail out 30 miles from the English coast when his plane caught fire. His wingman reported his chute never opened; however, he was picked up and suffered no more than two black eyes and a cut lip.

In August 1943, Lt. Colonel Chesley Peterson replaced Colonel Anderson to become Commander of the 4th, the youngest Colonel in the USAAC. In October he was promoted to full Colonel at the age of 23. He held the position of Group Commander until 1 January 1944, at which time the Command passed to fellow Eagle Donald Blakeslee. Pete was retired from flying duties, having completed 200 flying sorties, and left to serve as Combat Operations Officer for the 9th Air Force Headquarters.

Peterson was credited with seven enemy aircraft destroyed and was awarded medals, including the British Distinguished Service Order, Distinguished Flying Cross, the RAF Medallion, Distinguished Service Cross, Distinguished Service Medal, the French Legion of Honor, the Legion of Merit with Oak Leaf Cluster, the Air Medal with two Oak Leaf Clusters, the Purple Heart, and Theatre and Campaign medals. He stayed in the service until retirement as a Major General in 1965.

Colonel **EVERETT W. STEWART**

Colonel Stewart was a product of Abilene, Kansas, which was also the home of Dwight Eisenhower. He was a combat veteran of both the Pacific and European Theatres in WWII.

He flew his first combat mission 7 December 1941 at Pearl Harbor. He then flew in P-40 units from Wake and Midway Islands from February to September 1942. After 280 combat hours in the Pacific Theatre he was transferred to Europe and the 355th Fighter Group in December 1943. He became Commanding Officer in November 1944. In February 1945 he became Commanding Officer of the 4th Fighter Group.

Colonel Blakeslee, who was abrupt and forceful, and spent most of his energy flying and commanding the pilot organization, left most of the administration and non-flying personnel concerns to Major Clatanoff, which fostered considerable resentment from the enlisted personnel. Unlike Blakeslee, Col. Stewart felt responsible for all personnel in the group. He wanted a happy ship. He wanted his pilots to play hard and fly hard, and he wanted the G.I.s looked after. To this end, he replaced Clatanoff as Ground Exec. with Captain Kenneth G. Patton of Winchester, Virginia.

Soft spoken and with his firm desire to get along with others soon gave Col. Stewart the status of being the most liked Commanding Officer the group had ever had. His plane was named "Sunny VIII," and he had 10 ½ victories to his credit. He had flown 180 missions for 510 combat hours. He had earned the Silver Star, the DFC / 3OLC, and the AM / 6OLC. He died in February 1982.

Col. Sidney S. Woods Hq Squadron, Deputy Group CO (left) with Crew Chief R. Lonier and Armament Man R. Easley. Col. Woods was downed on April 16, 1945, and was a POW for 13 days. He was an Ace in the Pacific in P-40s and scored an additional five victories on 22 March 1945 in a P-51. *Konsler Collection*

Lt Colonel **SIDNEY S. WOODS**

Lt. Colonel Sidney Woods was born 25 July 1917 in San Marcos, Texas. He was raised in Arizona and played football for the University of Arizona, graduating in 1939. He joined the Army in the cavalry in 1939 and transferred to flight school, getting his wings in September 1941.

He was flying with the 49th Pursuit Group, USAAF, when the Japanese attacked Pearl Harbor. Based in the South Pacific, he flew P-38 Lightnings with the 479th Fighter Group, shooting down four Japanese aircraft during 112 combat missions. He returned to the States in 1943 and was soon assigned to the ETO flying P-38s. His tour completed, he again returned to the States, and again was sent to the ETO flying P-51 Mustangs with the 4th Fighter Group as Deputy Group Commander, becoming Group Commander 26 February 1945.

On 22 March, on an escort mission with 15th AF bombers from Italy, no enemy action was encountered. After their escort duties ended the Mustang pilots headed towards Berlin. They spotted 15 FW-190s loaded with bombs taking off from an airfield. They dove on the 190s and Sidney was lining up on the tail of one. When close behind the 190 he pulled the trigger to drop his wing tanks, but when only one jettisoned the drag on the other in the 109's slipstream caused his 51 to flip on its back. He fired from his inverted position and shot down the first Kraut. Meanwhile, a 190 was firing a deflection shot at him from above. He pulled up, fired, and flamed the second e/a. He went after a third, gave him a short squirt, and it crashed. He then went after another that was firing at a Mustang and destroyed it. He turned and chased a fifth e/a and, seeing his tracers miss, he adjusted his aim and with his remaining tracers he shot down his fifth for the day.

His Group shot down ten of the 190s in a battle which lasted a half hour and proved that the newer members of the group were quite capable in a testy combat situation.

On Sidney's 68th mission over Prague he was shot down by flak and became a POW *for thirteen days*! The European war ended, and he was sent home to the States and discharged in 1945.

He was called back to active duty in 1951-52, commanding a training unit. During this time he led the Air Force Jet Aerobatic Team. When finally discharged, he had 10 ½ victories and was honored with the Distinguished Service Cross, Silver Star, Distinguished Flying Cross with eight Oak Leaf Clusters, Air Medal with nine Oak Leaf Clusters, and the *Croix de Guerre*. He became a successful business man in Arizona and was active in politics. He died of cancer at the age of 71.

IV

334th Fighter Squadron

The 334th Fighter Squadron was the successor to No. 71 Eagle Squadron of the Royal Air Force when the Fourth Fighter Group was activated on 12 September 1942. They were based in Debden Field, Essex, England. The "Fighting Eagles," as they were called, flew Spitfires until the arrival of P-47 Thunderbolts in 1943. A year later they changed to P-51 Mustangs, their mounts until the end of the war. The 334th was the top scoring squadron of the three in the group with 395 kills.

After VE Day the squadron moved to the States to Andrews Air Force Base, MD, where they began flying jets. By November 1949 they were en route to Korea, where their designation was "334 Fighter Interceptor Squadron." They were credited with the destruction of 142.5 enemy aircraft.

They remained in the Far East until December 1957 when they were reassigned to Seymour Johnson Air Force Base in NC. They have participated in combat in all the major conflicts up to and including Operation Desert Storm.

In 1995, the 334th Fighter Interceptor Squadron mission changed to "Fighter Training Unit," training pilots for combat in F-15E Strike Eagles. Since 1995 they have trained over 500 pilots to fly and fight in this world premier multi-role fighter.

The "Fighting Eagles" Aces

Lieutenant **William Antonides**
Lt. Colonel **James W. Ayers**
Lt Colonel **Duane Willard Beeson**
Captain **Thomas R. Bell**
1st Lieutenant **Hipolitus T. Biel**
Lieutenant **Arthur Reed Bowers**
Major **Gerald Brown**
Colonel **Raymond C. Care**
Captain **Archie W. Chatterly**
Colonel **Oscar Coen**
Lt. Colonel **Gregory A. Daymond**
1st Lieutenant **Gordan A. Denson**
Captain **Victor France**
1st Lieutenant **Kenneth G. Helfrecht**
Major **Howard W. Hively**
Lieutenant **Ralph Kidd Hofer**
Captain **David W. Howe**
Captain **Joseph L. Lang**
Captain **Donald M. Malmsten**
Captain **Jack D. McFadden**
Major **Michael G. McPharlin**
Captain **Nicholas Megura**
Major **Henry L. Mills**
Major **Gerald Montgomery**
Lt. Colonel **Louis H. Norley**
Colonel **Steve N. (Spiro) Pisanos**
Captain **Carl G. Payne**
Captain **Alexander Rafalovich**
Lieutenant **Grover C. Siems Jr.**
Captain **William B. Smith**
Major **Winslow M. Sobanski**
Lieutenant **Frank E. Speer**
1st Lieutenant **William E. Whalen**
Captain **Vasseure H. Wynn**

Lt. **WILLIAM ANTONIDES**

Lt. Antonides, from Glenwood Springs, Colorado, was assigned to 334 Squadron, 4th Fighter Group in February 1945. He was combat-ready in time for a freelance on the 27th to Leipzig, Germany. That day the Group strafed Weimar Airdrome and destroyed 40 enemy aircraft with the loss of two. Antonides accounted for two of the enemy aircraft.

His next encounter was on 16 April. "A" Group struck Gablingen Airdrome near Augsburg, Germany, and "B" Group hit Praha/Kbely Airdrome near Prague. Both Groups found their airdromes loaded with enemy aircraft pulled back from the front for safety. Together, they destroyed an unprecedented 105 aircraft in spite of heavy flak concentrations. Antonides accounted for five e/a destroyed.

The victory was not without losses, however, with eight of our pilots and planes lost; two pilots killed and six becoming POWs. In addition, two were wounded and about 20 of our planes were damaged by the Germans' determined defenses.

The air war was rapidly coming to a close, and Antonides did not get any more chances to destroy enemy aircraft. In September he was transferred to the 10th Air Depot. He had earned an Air Medal and one Oak Leaf Cluster.

Lt Colonel **JAMES W. AYERS**

Jim was born in February 1925 in Tahlequah, Oklahoma, capital of the Cherokee Nation. His earliest recollection of his desire to become a flyer was when, in the ninth grade, he was asked to fill out a questionnaire on what he would like to be when he was an adult. His answer was very direct, "I want to be a fighter pilot in the Eagle Squadron."

At the age of 19 he enlisted in the Army Air Corps and became an Aviation Cadet, graduating in January 1944 at Foster Field,

Texas. He had the usual 10 hours in "war-weary" Curtis P-40s as the culmination of his training. Since he was Cadet CO of his squadron he was given an option as to where he would like to go for further training. He chose P-51s at Winter Haven, Florida. Upon completion of this training, his contingent was flown to England and put into a replacement pool. He soon was assigned to the 4th Fighter Group, 334 Squadron for his combat career.

He flew a tour, with three extensions, and was one of only two out of his pool of 15 replacements to survive and return to the States unscathed; the rest were killed or shot down to become POWs. Although Jim survived, his career was not without mishap. In July 1944 his engine conked out a couple of times on the way to the target. He couldn't get above 27,300 feet and got mixed up with some flak and decided to abort. When he came through the very low overcast he found he was lost. He saw a field and attempted to land but overshot. As he attempted to go around for another try his engine failed again and he went through a fence and turned over in a potato patch. He had other occasions where he had damage from flak but was able to stay right-side up in landing; the goal of all pilots.

At war's end he returned to the States by ship. He then joined a National Guard unit in Tulsa, Oklahoma, where he flew P-51s, F-84s, and F-86s. He later was called back to duty under the command of Colonel Peterson, an early CO of the 4th Fighter Group in England. The unit was scheduled to go to Korea but was, instead, sent to Europe as the 48th Fighter Wing based in Chaumont, France. There they lived in tents, quite a come-down from the delightful quarters they had occupied in the 4th Group in Debden, England.

Upon his return to the States he became an instructor pilot at a commercial field where duty kept him from 7:00 AM to 7:00 PM, generally seven days a week. His students were mostly wash-outs from Aviation Cadet training under the GI bill who felt they were really "Ace" material.

Again he was called back to duty during the Korean War where he flew B-52s.

After his tour he returned to the States, where he found time to go to the University of Tulsa, earning a degree in Business Administration, and to court a young lady he had met. They had a beautiful military wedding, complete with crossed sabers and military protocol. Their union produced two children to their delight, a boy and a girl. Jim subsequently bought a steel manufacturing plant "Prior Products," which he operated until retirement.

Jim had a mixed bag of nine enemy aircraft destroyed and earned the Distinguished Flying Cross and the Air Medal with 12-OLC. He is now retired and lives in Garland, Texas.

Lt Colonel **DUANE WILLARD BEESON**

Colonel Beeson of Boise, Idaho, had planned to become a lawyer. To obtain the money for his education he worked many jobs, including selling magazines, and eventually wound up as a hotel clerk in Oakland, California. He was small in stature but very aggressive and intense. Neat and fastidious in dress; dark-haired and handsome, he was the personification of the image of a fighter pilot.

He had drive and an analytical mind, and was meticulous about detail in any enterprise he undertook.

Being adventurous, he enlisted in the Royal Canadian Air Force in 1940 at the age of 19. Upon completing his training he was assigned to No. 71 Eagle Squadron of the British Royal Air Force in April 1942 and transferred to the newly-formed U.S. Army Air Force in September of the same year.

While in the RAF, Beeson enjoyed their policy of encouraging pilots to harass the enemy as much as possible. To this end he would arrange to fly with Roy Evans, from 121 Squadron, who enjoyed crossing the Channel and strafing targets of opportunity. "Bee" (as he came to be known) wanted to learn all he could about strafing, since he had developed an intense hatred of the Germans and wanted to kill them wherever and whenever he could. When he became part of the USAAF he found it next to impossible to obtain permission to cross the Channel to harass the Krauts, so he had to be content to go only on planned missions.

Beeson practiced deflection shooting with a passion and studied the techniques of successful great pilots of WWI. He was aggressive in his attacks on the enemy and developed his own style of combat. He believed in speed and was not afraid to overshoot his target. He would pounce with fury upon an enemy aircraft, firing from close range and overshooting with enough speed that he would not, himself, become a target. He became one of the deadliest pilots the 4th produced, and his rivalry with Don Gentile provided an example that motivated the other pilots of the group to excel. Beeson was an excellent pilot, very dependable, and always willing to learn.

Although he was the first Ace of 334 Squadron and became one of the top-scoring pilots of the 4th, he was quiet and did not seek publicity.

However, Bee could not escape notice anymore than he could escape the fact that he was aggressive and daring in the accomplishment of his duties. He was awarded the Distinguished Service Cross for extraordinary heroism while escorting bombers over Frankfurt, Germany. When diving to intercept *Luftwaffe* fighters about to attack the bombers, his squadron was in turn about to be attacked by six enemy aircraft from above; although his own plane was damaged, he and his wingman turned into the attack. With odds three-to-one they scattered the attackers. Beeson pursued the enemy and pressed his attack, destroying two and probably saving considerable damage to the bombers and fighters below.

Beeson, who was to be a Lt. Colonel at 26, had accumulated a score of 24 *Luftwaffe* planes destroyed. He was to succumb to the same fate as many of his predecessors, a calamity called flak. It came as he was strafing on a low-level mission with the 4th Group attacking four different airdromes on 4 April 1944. As might be expected flak found its target, cutting his coolant line, and Bee was headed for an extended stay as a guest of the Third Reich.

Hanns Scharff, the *Luftwaffe's* master interrogator, was not without a sense of humor. On occasion he was capable of arranging unusual preludes to his interrogation of special prisoners. Beeson was one marked for a special welcome. After spending an extended length of time in solitary confinement Bee was summoned. Hanns assembled several of Beeson's fellow 4th Fighter Group detainees on a friendly basis in his office. Being together, the group became somewhat boisterous as they awaited the reason for this unusual gathering. Scharff wrote the name Major Beeson on his desk pad and they almost went wild. Bee had been their Squadron Commander, and they were overjoyed to discover he had lived through the crash of his plane.

There was a knock at the door, Scharff said "Come in," and there stood Beeson, frozen at attention, with his eyes looking straight forward. His friends cheered loudly as he saluted. Scharff rose from his chair and said "Major, come in and say hello to your buddies." Beeson took a step forward, still looking straight ahead, and said, "I do not know any of these gentlemen." They shouted encouragement to him as he still refused to recognize them. "Sorry gentlemen, I do not know who you are." Soon the odds against him were too great and he joined the crowd. Scharff soon became convinced Beeson would not cooperate, so he sent him to a Stalag in Oberursel.

The noses of the 4th Group planes had been painted a distinctive red, and when Bee was able to send mail he sent a card to his Commanding Officer, which was shown to General Jesse Auton, Commander of the 65th Fighter Wing in England, "Colonel, they know all about us over here—*paint the entire plane red!*"

Beeson had flown Hurricanes, Spitfires, P-47s, and P-51s in combat, was credited with 24 enemy destroyed, and spent 13 months in Stalag Luft I, Barth, Germany. He had awards from the U.S., Britain, France, Canada, and Belgium, including the Distinguished Service Cross, the Distinguished Flying Cross with six OLC, the Silver Star, the Air Medal with five OLC, the Purple Heart, the Belgian *Croix de Guerre*, and the Distinguished Unit Citation. He remained in the USAAF after WWII until his tragic death in 1947 of a brain tumor at the age of 26. He is buried in Arlington National Cemetery.

Captain **THOMAS R. BELL**

Captain Bell was from Shawboro, NC, and was assigned to the 4th Fighter Group, 334 Squadron, on 28 September 1944, where he remained until the end of the war.

He became Assistant Operations and Gunnery Officer in March 1945.

Bell had five and one half enemy planes destroyed.

1Lt **HIPOLITUS T. BIEL**

Hipolitus Biel was born July 28, 1916, of Polish immigrant parents in St. Paul, Minnesota. In 1936 he applied to the United States Army Air Corps to enter their pilot training program. Unable to meet all of their strict entrance guidelines he applied to the Royal Canadian Air Force, and on 5 August 1941 he was enlisted. He trained in de Havilland Tiger Moth biplanes and AT-6 Harvards, graduating as a Sergeant Pilot on 24 July 1942.

After a two week leave "Tom" reported to Halifax, Nova Scotia, for transport to England, where he arrived 18 August. There he trained in Miles Masters and Spitfires and finished on 7 March. He then applied for and received a discharge and transferred to the U.S. Army Air Force as a Flight Officer. On 7 September he was assigned to the 4th Fighter Group, 334 Squadron flying P-47s.

He was a steady and effective pilot, destroying 11.3 enemy aircraft, one or two at a time over seven months. He was promoted to 2nd Lieutenant in January 1944 and 1st Lieutenant in February.

He had a very unusual incident on 29 March 1944. Lt. Colonel Clark was leading a Target Withdrawal Support over France.

Near Gifhorn, 30 plus enemy aircraft attacked the bombers from the northeast while fifteen attacked from the south. The 4th bounced both groups and combat ranged from 18,000 feet to the deck. Biel was busy chasing several 190s, getting hits on one. He chased it around a small town and damaged it severely, setting it on fire as its belly tank blew up. They flew through a snow storm and as they came out, Biel was beside the Kraut looking at him face to face. Biel fell back and fired, doing more damage, and then flew up on the right side of the 190, looking to see if the German was still alive. They looked at each other, and Biel again positioned himself for more firing. Soon the 190 was on fire from nose to tail and the German prepared to bail. However, he was too low and Biel flew close formation to him as he made a perfect belly landing in a snow-covered field.

Flames engulfed the plane and flak was intense, so Tom climbed for altitude and headed for base, not knowing whether or not the Hun had survived.

Biel was KIA when he was shot down in aerial combat 24 April 1944. He had 11.3 enemy aircraft destroyed and had earned the Distinguished Flying Cross and the Air Medal with an Oak Leaf Cluster.

2nd Lieutenant **ARTHUR REED BOWERS**

Lt. Bowers was from Tiskilwa, IL, and was assigned to the 4th Fighter Group, 334 Squadron, 16 November 1944. He remained there until the end of the war.

He flew a P-51 QP-S named "Sweet Arlene." He was credited with six enemy aircraft and earned the Air Medal with one Oak Leaf Cluster, as well as the Purple Heart.

Major **GERALD BROWN**

Major (Jerry) Brown was born 2 December 1917 in Globe, Arizona. He joined the United States Army on 6 December 1941, the day before Pearl Harbor, and served in the enlisted ranks until June 1942, when he became an Aviation Cadet. He graduated in March 1943, and began an interesting career flying with different groups throughout the various conflict venues.

He was first assigned to the 55th Fighter Group, 38th Fighter Squadron in England in September 1943. He scored his first victory in January 1944 near Venlo, Holland. He was promoted to Captain in March and became an Ace in April, downing a Fw-190 and a He-111 over Munster.

When he finished his tour he served as a P-38 replacement training unit operations officer. Bored with this duty, he sought a combat mission and was assigned to the 4th Fighter Group, 334 Squadron, where he flew P-51s. He became acting Squadron Commanding Officer in July 1944. On 5 September, leading a flight on an escort mission to Karlsruhe, his plane began to trail smoke and lose altitude at 21,000 feet. At 10,000 feet he jettisoned his canopy and announced his intention to bail out, at which point one of the other pilots asked, "Are you taking your section with you?" He then pulled up, rolled over, and went into a spin. He recovered, rolled over, and bailed out at about 5.000 feet. His plane dove vertically into the ground, exploding on contact. His wingman flew over and saw he was safe, standing by his chute waving. He evaded German patrols and was returned to Debden the next day by the French underground, but not until he had been toasted with champagne for being the first American into the village of Bucquoy! Four days later he was back leading a support mission to Mainz.

As a Lieutenant Colonel, when the Korean War broke out he was made Commander of the 39th Fighter Group in Japan. In July 1950 he led ground support missions and was eventually shot down by Chinese ground fire in November. He spent three years as a POW and was released in September 1953. He was promoted to Colonel in 1958 and served in various command and staff assignments until he retired in 1967. Colonel Brown had destroyed 5 enemy aircraft and received the Distinguished Service Medal, the Legion of Merit, the Distinguished Flying Cross with four OLC, the Bronze Star, the Air Medal with 13 OLC, and the French *Croix de Guerre*.

Colonel **RAYMOND C. CARE**

15 April 1944: Captain Care was leading the 4th Group on a jackpot operation to Juterbog Aerodrome in Germany when bad weather forced the Group to split up into small sections. These sections then attacked three different aerodromes in small groups. Captain Care and Lt. Biel attacked an unidentified field northeast of Celle and shared in the destruction of a Ju-52. Care's plane was hit by flak and he had to bail out.

Ray was from Angola, Indiana, 27 years old, and had come to England in March 1942. He had been in No.71 Eagle Squadron of the RAF before transferring to the 4th Fighter Group, 334 Squadron upon its inception. When he was shot down he became the third Commanding Officer of 334 Squadron to be lost in a month. He had seven confirmed and one probable enemy aircraft destroyed to his credit prior to being shot down.

When Ray landed in his parachute he was immediately picked up by German civilians. They even helped him out of his chute. He was put in solitary confinement in an interrogation center for seven days on bread and water, without cigarettes or any such luxuries as a bath. After interrogation he was transferred to a permanent camp near the Polish border. In January, the Russians broke out of the Warsaw area and were nearing the camp. The Germans decided to move the prisoners out rather than have the Russians free them. With one hour of notice the 2,000 prisoners were on the road. He later wrote:

"We left hurriedly in zero weather, with a severe snow storm whipping at us, with only what we could carry on our backs. We force marched for two nights and three days, with no sleep and only the food from Red Cross packages, which the Germans had hurriedly issued to us. We carried what food we could, but there was no way to prepare any of it; all we could do was munch on a chocolate bar or a biscuit now and then if we had any. Many of the men went completely off the beam and started breaking out of the ranks to just wander off into the wood. Those of us who still had our reason would pull them back into the line to keep the guards from shooting them. The march was a complete snafu and a thorough going mess.

"On the third day they herded us into a pottery factory for a rest. I took off my shoes and socks and the skin from my instep to my toes came off with my socks. For two days I could not wear my shoes and I hobbled around in my stocking feet in the biting cold. We drained some hot water from a boiler in the factory and were able to make some instant coffee; that was a delight.

"The Germans again marched us, two more days and then loaded us into French 40-and-8s, fifty or more to a car and shipped us like cattle to Nuremburg. We spent four days and nights in those stinking, overcrowded cars. Most of us were sick with dysentery or had frostbitten feet and fingers and badly needed medical attention.

"At Nuremburg we were moved into an ex-Italian camp which had no mattresses and a shortage of bunks. The place was infested with bed-bugs and lice and was absolutely filthy. There were no baths, and only two water taps for the 450 men in the three barracks; it was not unusual to wait in a queue for an hour to wash my face and hands. For six weeks, we lived on a seventh of a loaf of bread and two small potatoes per man, per day. It was February and there was no fuel for heat. Finally Red Cross parcels arrived and we had some relief from the starvation diet.

"By 1 April, the American army was approaching and they decided to again move us, this time towards Munich. Four of us decided, on the first night, to slip away from the column and strike out for the American lines. We had three blankets for the four of us and a little food. We walked by night and slept hidden in barns or in the woods during the day for eleven nights. Our food ran out after four days and we lived on mangel beets which we dug up by hand from the earth mounds at the edge of fields.

"This cow-food kept us from starving as we trudged along in an almost constant rain which kept us soaked to the skin. Finally, we spotted a barn and we decided to take a chance, being so weak and exhausted we no longer cared what might happen. We slept in the hay-mow two nights and a day, resting up until a peasant woman came into the barn with a little terrier. The dog promptly raised an alarm and the woman hurried off to summon German troops. Soon some SS Troops came and surrounded the barn so we gave ourselves up and were turned over to the civilian police force. We were kept in a military barracks and then started south on another march with about 20 others who had escaped much as we had and were subsequently picked up. One of the guards was a lieutenant who used to live in New Jersey, and I kidded him that I would have that fancy dress pistol he was wearing.

"After three or four days, two of our company got sick and I began to talk Geneva Convention stuff to the Lieutenant in charge and said I would hold him responsible if these men died for lack of proper hospitalization and that we would not go a bit further, so we camped at a barn for another couple of days. We saw many German troops obviously retreating. I kept reminding the lieutenant about his pistol and then told him they better make a big white flag. That night he made a flag which we stuck up at the edge of town and waited. Soon we saw American jeeps and trucks and as soon as the lieutenant was convinced they were really Americans, he calmly reached down and took off his pistol and handed it to me. Thus armed and with two German prisoners, we met the column and turned our prisoners over to the Americans and surrendered the town."

Ray Care and his friends got to Paris for a couple of days and he then returned to England. Back at the base, now at Steeple Morden, he told about his interrogation. He had been handed a "Red Cross" form to fill out with a whole page full of questions, such as name, rank, serial number, Wing, Group, Squadron, call sign for the day, and many more questions totally unrelated to the Red Cross. He filled out his name, rank, and serial number and returned it to the interrogator, who said in perfect English, "Surely you're not done already." Ray said that was it and the interrogator laughed and said, "I'll fill it out for you," which he promptly did from memory. There was a little more chit chat and then he was sent to the permanent camp, where he became just another "Kriegie."

Ray also told of a fellow in the interrogation camp who showed him a statement, sworn to by a *Luftwaffe* officer concerning an RAF tail gunner. The gunner had bailed out of a burning Halifax bomber at 18,000 feet without his chute, which also was on fire. He figured he would rather die from the fall than burn to death. He passed out on the way down and regained consciousness in a pine forest. He had landed in snow covered branches which, one-by-one broke his fall and he didn't have a scratch on him.

Raymond Care retired from the USAF as a Colonel in 1963 with the Distinguished Flying Cross with two Oak Leaf Clusters and the Air Medal with two Oak Leaf Clusters. He then worked in Civil Service at Kelly Air Base, Texas, until retiring. He died in San Antonio in April 1987.

Captain **ARCHIE W. CHATTERLY**

Archie was from San Diego, California, and joined the 4th Fighter Group, 334 Squadron on 20 January 1943. He flew a P-47 named "California or Bust." His tour was not without negative incidents.

His normal combat routine was first interrupted by a mid-air collision on 27 April 1943. He was flying a P-47 in a mock dogfight over Castle Camps with Lt. James Wilkinson. Archie overshot, slicing off Wilkinson's tail. Wilkinson bailed out, but was unconscious with back injuries when he hit the ground. The injuries kept him hospitalized for months. Archie, however, was able to dead-stick his plane near New Market.

Almost a year later, on 6 March 1944 Col. Don Blakeslee led the Group, flying Mustangs, on a Target Support Mission to Berlin. Archie's section chased six Me-109s and he then attacked an Me-110, interrupting its attack on a lone Fort. After downing this enemy aircraft he went after an Me-210 closing on the tail of another Mustang, causing it to crash.

He then joined three other Mustangs as they were heading home when an Fw-190 made a pass on them, but Major Hank Mills put an end to its pilot's career.

Again they headed for home flying line abreast. Nature called Archie, and he was in the midst of utilizing the pilot's relief tube just in time to see tracers pass on each side of him. The section broke and Lt. Godfrey destroyed the intruder. Back at Debden, they found four machine-gun holes in Archie's stabilizer, two in the prop, a canon hole in the port aileron, and machine-gun holes ripping the underside of the starboard wing. That was a potential catastrophe resulting from a lapse of concentration on priorities in a combat area.

Archie's next misfortune occurred on 27 March 1944 on a mission to Bordeaux. He had downed an Me-109 but was hit by flak from towers and barges on the shore of Lake Biscarosse, forcing him to bail out. He became a POW one week after being appointed Squadron Operations Officer.

In spite of these misfortunes, Archie had 5.5 enemy aircraft destroyed and had been awarded the Distinguished Flying Cross with one Oak Leaf Cluster, the Air Medal with two Oak Leaf Clusters, and the POW Medal.

Colonel **OSCAR COEN**

Oscar Coen was born in Wallum, North Dakota, 11 May 1917. He spent his boyhood on a Wisconsin dairy farm where he won a 4H championship with a huge Holstein bull. He graduated from the University of Wisconsin at Madison with a Bachelor of Science degree.

He had become a school teacher in Marion, Illinois, but he decided he wanted to fly, and in May 1940 he enrolled as a U.S. Army Aviation Cadet. He soon discovered that he was to become a Navigator and resigned, at the age of 23 (Sept 1940), and joined the Royal Canadian Air Force, where he had to drink a quart of water in order to reach the minimum weight requirements for enlistment.

After completing his Royal Canadian Air Force training and his Operational Training Unit program in England he was assigned to No. 71 Eagle Squadron, RAF, consisting of U.S. volunteers flying Hurricanes. These were soon replaced with Spitfires armed with cannons.

On 20 October 1941 Oscar was strafing a train which blew up under him and he was forced to bale out over French occupied territory. With the help of the French Underground, dressed as a teenage boy, he was able to avoid capture and to escape through Southern France and Spain to Gibraltar. He returned to his Squadron on Christmas Day 1941.

Back on Ops, on 27 April 1942 Coen and Mike McPharlin cooperated in downing three Fw-190s. On 19 August 1942 the two again collaborated in downing a Ju-88 and a "probable," and Oscar destroyed an Fw-190 while helping to maintain air superiority over "Operation Jubilee," the code name for the Dieppe landing. Unfortunately, McPharlin's Spitfire was badly damaged and he had to bail out over the Channel. He was rescued by a launch and returned to his Squadron.

On 15 September 1942 Coen transferred to the U.S. Army Air Corps as a Captain and was subsequently introduced to the P-47 Thunderbolt. In that aircraft he became an Ace, downing his sixth enemy aircraft and three probables. Prior to obtaining the P-47s, the Eagles in the Army Air Corps continued flying Spitfires maintained by British crews, since there were not enough P-47s available for an entire group and too few crews were trained in their maintenance. They did, however, personalize their Spitfires by painting Army Air Force stars over the British roundels.

The transition was not easy, to say the least.

The Jug weighed in at seven tons, compared to a Spit at half that weight. Being a new design, the Jugs had many problems to be ironed out. It did not pull out of a dive as nimbly as a Spit, which caused a couple of pilots to crash. At high altitude engines could blow up or freeze, and it was difficult for pilots to exit the plane in an emergency.

Oscar had a catastrophe; his engine exploded, and in bailing out at high speed he used his right arm to pull the rip cord, and the sudden force fractured and dislocated his shoulder. Fortunately, he was over England and received immediate attention and therapy that saved his arm. There followed a two month leave for recuperation, and then he was back to the group on 4 August 1943. Still unable to raise his right arm above his head, he had to modify some of his movements to comply with the demands of cockpit routine, but he managed to the extent that he was again able to lead a squadron into combat.

On 11 April 1944 he was assigned to headquarters of the 8th USAF in London. There he participated in planning fighter cover for the impending invasion of the continent. On D-Day he flew a P-47 over the landing areas to observe the results of the planning.

During the war Oscar accumulated 550 combat hours on 200 missions and is credited with 5.5 enemy aircraft destroyed. He flew Spitfires, Thunderbolts, and Mustangs. On VJ-Day Oscar was back in the United States, attached to the Pentagon and assigned to Continental Air Command, Fighter Branch of Training, as a full Colonel at the age of 27.

His awards included three Silver Stars, the British Distinguished Flying Cross, the Royal Air Force Medallion, the Campaign Medal of the Battle of Britain, the *Croix de Guerre*, the U.S. Air Medal with three Oak Leaf Clusters, three Distinguished Flying Crosses, and Campaign and Service Medals. Oscar remarked he never worked on nor was he awarded the Good Conduct Medal.

Oscar remained in the Air Force in many different capacities in ROTC, Air National Guard, as a Jet Fighter Commander, and as a Wing Deputy Commander for Operations in the Air Force. He retired in 1962 as a Colonel and took up ranching in eastern Oregon. After the war he married a Canadian girl, Virginia, the widow of his best friend Michael McPharlin, who was killed on D-Day, and he adopted Michael's daughter Carleen.

Unfortunately, when Oscar enlisted in the RCAF he inadvertently had taken the oath expected of all entering the RCAF, affirming allegiance to the King of England. Even after transferring to the United States Army Air Force and serving until retirement as a Colonel he never realized that he was no longer a U.S. citizen. It was not until the 1960s that he discovered this upon applying for a passport and having his request denied. He was not alone in this predicament, and eventually Congress officially reinstated those who had been expatriated for the same reason.

Colonel Coen died 23 June 2004 at Iowa State Veterans Home in Boise.

Lt. Colonel **GREGORY A. DAYMOND**

Born in Great Falls, Montana, in November 1920, Gregory soon became known as Gus, from his middle name Augustus. He grew up in California, and upon graduating from high school he worked in the motion picture industry in various positions. He took flying lessons on the side and qualified as a private pilot at 16. When the war broke out in Europe he joined the RAF, went to OTU in England, and eventually was assigned to No.71 Eagle Squadron.

While flying Hurricanes, he shot down his first Me-109 over France in July 1941. In the same month he shot down a second Me-109, followed by a Do-17 in August. In early September, flying a Spitfire, he shot down another 109, and later in the month he became an Ace by destroying his fifth enemy aircraft, another 109, over Dunkirk, possibly becoming the first Allied Ace in WWII.

Gus was sent to the States in December on a lecture tour and returned to combat in June 1942. In August he was promoted to Commander of No.71 Eagle Squadron. In September 1942 the Eagle Squadrons were transferred to the United States Army Air Force, where he received a commission as a Major. By then he had a record of seven enemy aircraft destroyed and was appointed Commander of 4th Fighter Group, 334th Squadron.

Eventually he was returned to the States to develop a combat indoctrination program for the USAAF. In November 1945 Gus left the service and returned to the movie industry. He obtained a degree in Physics from Cal Tech and entered the aerospace industry, leaving in 1957 to join Interstate Electronics Corporation, from which he retired in 1987.

Daymond became a Lt. Colonel in the United States Army Air Force Reserve. He had flown Hurricanes, Spitfires, and P-47s, and was awarded the British Distinguished Flying Cross with Bar by King George.

1st Lieutenant **GORDON A. DENSON**

From Rockville, CT, Gordon was assigned to the 4th Fighter Group, 334 Squadron, 23 January 1945. He stayed there until 21 September when he was transferred to the 64th Fighter Wing. He had flown 24 missions in P-51 QP-E named "Priscilla."

Gordon had five enemy aircraft to his credit and was awarded the Air Medal with three Oak Leaf Clusters, the Air Force Commendation Medal, the Air Force Meritorious Service Medal, and the Freedom Foundation Honor Medal.

He retired from the United States Air Force with the rank of Colonel.

Captain **VICTOR FRANCE**

Victor France was from Dallas, Texas, and he appropriately named his P-47 and later his P-51 "Miss Dallas." The nose art was a nude, her intimate parts covered by a large Texas cowboy hat, standing in front of a map of Texas and brandishing a six-gun. Vic came from the British No. 71 Eagle Squadron, and on 7 August 1942 was ushered into the 4th Fighter Group, 334th Squadron when the U.S. Group became operational. Vic always served aggressively, chalking up victories, and with his leadership abilities soon became "C" Flight Commanding Officer on 21 March 1944.

Vic was impressive looking, with his six foot height and wide shoulders surmounting a narrow waist and athletic chest. These features were enhanced by his custom-tailored British uniform, the jacket lined in crimson silk. His trousers were tailored slim and just short enough to show a glimpse of his highly-polished, high-heeled, narrow-toed Texas cowboy boots. He walked with a slow and relaxed amble, and when he entered a room every female eye was immediately drawn to him. He was well known by the girls from the famed Windmill Theatre, who were his favorite escorts whenever he was in London.

As he climbed into his cockpit, his impressive good looks were enhanced by a polka dot scarf tied Ascot style around his neck. To complete the image he was a splendid pilot. Strafing on the deck was no stranger to his tactics. On one occasion, he flew so low while strafing a railroad engine that as it blew up the bottom of his P-51 was covered with soot, and a German newspaper was subsequently retrieved from his air scoop.

Unfortunately, all his charm and skill were unable to prevent his death in combat as he doggedly pursued a Nazi fighter determined to destroy a lone, stricken B-17. It was on 18 April, and the Group's escort duty was finished. Fuel and ammunition

were running low. Group Commander Colonel Blakeslee ordered the Group to return to base. Vic could not leave the injured bomber to be consumed by the Messerschmitts attacking it. Followed by his wingman, he dove into the pack of Germans, dispersing them and shooting at one that attacked his wingman, driving him off. However one Kraut persisted, returning to peck away at the bomber, causing Vic to announce over the radio, "The rest of you guys go home, I'm gonna get that bastard."

When Vic attacked the 109 did a split-s, with Vic on his tail in a vertical dive. Vic was scoring hits as the two were nearing compressibility. Unable to pull out of the dive, Vic hit the ground in a ball of flames, his plane disintegrating over a wide area. Shortly a second searing flash arose nearby, as the escaping 109, at hedge level, came under the avenging fire of Lt. Nick Megura.

Vic had 8.66 enemy aircraft destroyed to his credit. He had earned the Distinguished Flying Cross with two Oak Leaf Clusters, the Air Medal with one Oak Leaf Cluster, and the Purple Heart. He had flown combat in Spitfires, Thunderbolts, and Mustangs.

The Windmill Girls mourned his demise.

Years later, it was discovered that Victor had met and become enamored of a young woman pilot who was ferrying P-51s to the 4th Group. When he died, Victor could not have known that he had fathered a child, a girl. Unfortunately, her mother also died when her daughter was only months old, and the infant child was raised by her grandmother, who kept her father's identity a secret. Upon the grandmother's death the young woman, Kathleen, discovered her father's identity while going through her grandmother's belongings. She wrote to Vic's former Commanding Officer, Col. Don Blakeslee, asking for information about her father. Blakeslee, in turn, contacted Don Allen, Vic's crew chief, and asked him to follow up on her request. Allen was able to send her several pictures and to give her much insight into Vic's life as a fighter pilot. She was delighted to learn about him.

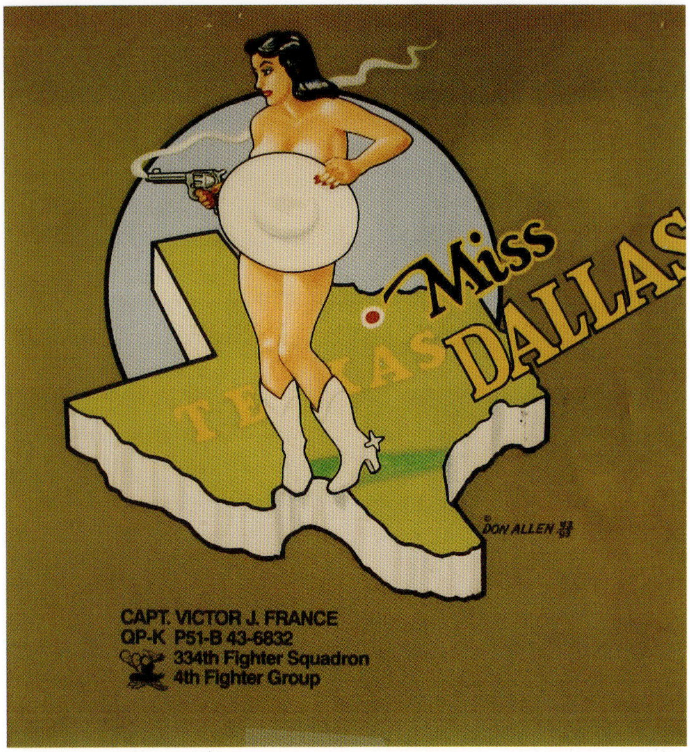

Don was astounded when her subsequent letters revealed that, although neither her father nor her mother (both P-51 pilots) could have known, Kathleen also was a pilot. She flew *in P-51s* as an attraction in air shows.

What a family coincidence! Could there be a P-51 gene?

1st Lt. **Kenneth G. Helfrecht**

Kenneth was born 19 February 1925, the third and last child of German-American parents. His father, a chemical engineer, died when he was seven, and his mother worked as many as three jobs at a time to raise him and his two siblings. Eventually, following Kenneth, all three children entered the armed forces; his sister in the Medical Corps, and his brother in the Army Signal Corps.

Kenneth enlisted in the Army Air Corps Reserve at the age of 18, and three months later was called up and qualified for single engine pilot training. He began his training as a Cadet in the class of 44A at Maxwell Field, Alabama. There he learned the usual prerequisites of a flying career: walking tours, eating square meals, and being constantly harassed by upper classmen. He contracted viral pneumonia and spent seven weeks in the base hospital. During this time he managed to learn how to run the floor polisher, and he fell in love with his ward nurse.

The hospital delay caused him to miss his training in 44A and he was assigned to class 44C. He went to a private flying training school near Douglas, Georgia. There he soloed and successfully ground-looped a Stearman PT-17, which did nothing to endear him to his instructor.

There followed Christmas at Basic in Macon, Georgia, where he learned to drink rum and coke with the inevitable hangover, meanwhile learning the vagaries of the BT-13 Vultee "Vibrator." Next, at Advanced in Jackson, Mississippi, he flew AT-6s and became acquainted with Dutch Indonesian B-25 pilots and their unusual use of bar soap as a deodorant. This may possibly have been the origin of the later popular "stick deodorant."

Helfrecht received his wings in March 1944, but had to wait six months before being assigned overseas. His duties kept him in Florida bases where he flew P-40s, learned how to swim, and upgraded his drinking to gin and tonic.

Finally overseas, at Goxhill, England, he was introduced to the P-51 and joined a group of 10 pilots destined to become replacements in the 4th Fighter Group. There, assigned to 334 Squadron, he had to learn some British routines and traditions left over from the Eagle Squadron days, and the new-to-him gyro gunsight. On his second mission, his flight leader took off after an Me-109, and in Ken's confusion amidst R/T screaming and tracers passing him he pulled up and saw a bandit about 600 yards away; he pressed the tit to fire, forgetting that the British button was not in the same location as he was used to finding it in his U.S. training, and consequently, nothing happened. He followed the enemy into a cloud bank and, seeing a plane vaguely, he fired; fortunately he missed, since it was one of ours.

In his subsequent 57 missions he never again fired at a plane in flight; consequently, by the grace of God, no one got hurt.

On 16 April 1945 things changed; with a routine escort of bombers to Rosenheim led by Major Norley successfully completed, the Group turned its attention to Gablingen Aerodrome and strafed for approximately 40 minutes. The field had moderate accurate flak, but the group continued to strafe the planes, many of which were parked in holes or bomb craters. The Group claimed 42 enemy aircraft destroyed and many damaged with no loss and only slight damage to four of our planes. Ken accounted for five of the *Luftwaffe* planes, thus becoming an Ace in a single day.

After four more uneventful missions, hostilities ceased and Kenneth returned home in mid-November. He returned to the University of Wisconsin, with tuition at $48 a semester, to pursue a degree in engineering. He managed to enjoy himself thoroughly but his grades suffered, so even with an extra semester to beef up his grade point average to qualify for grad school he was unsuccessful.

In June 1950 he began employment at Commonwealth Telephone Company, where he served 37 years as an engineer. In 1959 he met a fellow employee who was beautiful and of an appropriate faith. They tied the knot in May. The union produced two children and eventually four grandchildren. He retired in 1987, his only regret being that he did not spend as much time with his family as he would have liked.

He never, however, regretted that exciting day at Gablingen, nor the Air Medal with five Oak Leaf Clusters that he had earned in combat.

Major **HOWARD W. HIVELY**

Howard Hively hailed from Columbus, Ohio, and Norman, Oklahoma. He was pursuing an engineering degree at the University of Oklahoma, and while studying economic geology became interested in the possibility of discovering oil deposits from studying aerial photographs. He worked with his professor, Dr. Melton, in pursuing this concept. Dr. Melton paid plane rental for Hively to fly and take aerial photographs.

While becoming interested in oil leases and attempting to form an aero-exploration firm, he saw a poster in a Dallas hotel inviting Americans to join the RAF's Eagle Squadrons. He applied, was accepted, and was sent to Baker's Field, California, for fighter pilot training. Baker's Field had civilian instructors and unmarked AT-6 planes. This was a handy device fitting well into Howard's social life. They provided thrilling transport for young women he might want to impress with an evening at some distant place.

Howard, who became known as "Deacon," loved to buzz whenever he could. One night, he went on a buzzing expedition with a local hotel as his target. The field's CO, who lived on the fifth floor, had to look down to see this activity and was quite upset, but was unable to identify the perpetrator.

Deacon fortunately shipped out and arrived in England 1 September 1941, and was assigned to No.71 Eagle Squadron. In September 1942 he was transferred to the U.S. 4th Fighter Group. In June 1943 he was ordered to Tangmere to cover a strike against German sub pens at St Nazaire. "Class A uniforms will be worn." This impressed the British Allies, "Do you always wear those uniforms on a mission?" The answer, of course, was, "What else."

After an unexciting mission, at the appointed time the Jugs headed for home. Suddenly, for no apparent reason, Deacon's cockpit became very hot and his shoes started to burn. At this point he discovered his plane was on fire. While debating his next move his prop stopped turning, thus forcing a rapid decision. He didn't relish spending time wet and cold in a dinghy, but being over the Channel, he had no choice. He abandoned his burning ship with his parachute swinging wildly in the wind.

During his descent he decided to get rid of any extraneous equipment. He hated to get rid of his pearl-handled revolver, a beauty his father had given him when he went off to war. The sudden realization that he had never fired the pistol led him to fire all six shots before giving it the heave-ho. When he hit the water he couldn't believe how deep the Channel was, but gasping for air he finally surfaced. He battled his wildly bucking dinghy, finally reaching the safety of its cold wet interior.

Hours later, when he felt he was slowly turning to ice, a launch appeared manned by men trained in revitalizing such lost souls. An eight-handed massage, warm clothes, and a shot of 180-proof rum did wonders for his morale as they headed for Portsmouth. Arriving in a turtle-neck sweater and grey flannel pants, he thought, "So much for my 'Class A' uniform."

On 6 June 1944 Deacon was promoted to CO of 334 Squadron, which incidentally coincided with D-Day. On 22 June the "Shuttle Run" to Russia and Italy took place. The first leg from Debden to Russia was 2200 miles, a seven-and-a-half-hour trek for the 48 fighters that were to escort 104 bombers over their target, Ruhland. They were then to continue on to Russia, where the fighters were to land at Poltava, and the bombers at other bases with suitable runways and facilities. Unbelievably, with all the difficulties this mission presented, including the lack of valid maps of the eastern end of the flight, Col. Blakeslee brought the Group in to the field, missing his ETA by only one minute.

Immediately upon landing Blakeslee was whisked off to some higher headquarters, leaving the Group under the command of Hively, who had been designated as 2nd in command. Hively then had the task of assigning quarters, taking care of the planes, and attending to the Russian protocol, all without the help of an interpreter. To make matters worse, the Germans had followed the Mustangs and mounted a bombing raid in the middle of the night. In the dark, the pilots took advantage of all possible protective devices regardless of whether they were slit trenches or "sanitary facilities." Some rather smelly, but glad to be alive, pilots emerged after the raid was concluded.

During their stay the Russians could not do enough to welcome the Americans. They were wined with copious amounts of vodka, dined with some rather questionable choices of food, and entertained with music and dance. Both Russian men and women of all ranks joined in the festivities.

On the 26th they had a mission to Drohobycz, Poland, and then continued on to Lucera, Italy. On 2 July, on a mission to Budapest, the Group was attacked by 75 Me-109s. In the bitter ensuing battle Hively shot down one Me-109. In turn his canopy was hit by a 20mm shell, badly injuring his right eye. Deacon persisted, using his left eye, to shoot down two more 109s before breaking off and returning to base, where he was hospitalized for his injuries.

On 5 July, with the Group returning to Debden, Deacon went AWOL from the Italian hospital in order to return with them. They flew from Salinas, Italy, to escort bombers over Beziers, France,

and then on to Debden to complete the third leg of this 6,000 mile triangle. The completed shuttle from England to Russia, to Italy, and back to England took the Group over ten countries, and consumed 29 hours of operational time. Needless to say, the free beer in the Officer's Club was quaffed with gusto and the tall tales waxed even taller as the evening wore on.

In October Hively was awarded the Distinguished Service Cross for heroism in the Budapest battle, where he and two others heroically attacked over 40 enemy fighters and pursued them with skill and perseverance in spite of the overwhelming odds.

In August 1944 he became Deputy Group and Station CO. Deacon served continuously from 1 September 1941 until the end of the war in 1945, with only one leave of 2-1/2 months in late 1944. He was credited with 14.5 enemy aircraft destroyed. He was awarded the Distinguished Service Cross, the Distinguished Flying Cross with six OLC, the Air Medal with seven OLC, and the Purple Heart.

He retired to West Virginia and spent most of his time traveling throughout the States visiting his old friends from the Fourth. He drove with practically everything he owned in his car, staying with his old buddies until his welcome wore out.

While visiting one in Florida in 1982, he accidentally fell out of the boat they were using to see the sights and died of a heart attack before he could be rescued.

Lt **RALPH KIDD HOFER**

Ralph Kidd Hofer was born Ralph Halbrook on a farm near Salem, Missouri, in 1921. Upon his father's death, when Ralph was only four, his mother remarried and his name was changed to Ralph Kidd Hofer. Eventually the name "Kidd" stuck with him throughout his combat career.

He was a very colorful character, and much has been written about him, both fact and fiction. However, having known him and flown with him, my research and separation of fact from fiction has been easy. Although he was capable and intelligent, he attached a very low priority to school work. Nevertheless, he managed to graduate from high school. He loved the outdoors, animals, and sports. He found great pleasure in riding horses, playing baseball and football, and boxing. He drifted naturally into semi-pro football and boxing. In 1940 he won a trophy in a Golden Gloves tournament as a light heavyweight. Meanwhile, he worked as a civilian at Fort Leonard Wood. Always mobile, he heard of good purses being paid in American Legion bouts in California. He arranged with a promoter to pick up a new Hudson in Detroit and delivered it to him in California in return for his travel expenses.

As the story goes, while waiting for the car to be finished he crossed over to Windsor, Ontario, Canada, on a lark. A border patrolman, assuming he was attempting to join the Royal Canadian Air Force, directed him to the recruiting station. Hofer had no interest in airplanes or flying, but he was caught up in the exuberance of the applicants he found there, and he immediately enlisted. He soon became addicted to flying. When he graduated from flying training he visited Chicago, where he was solicited to appear in a billboard promotion for Coca-Cola. He was handsome, powerfully built, with a perpetual smile, and looked great in his RCAF uniform. Posing with a U.S. cadet, he personified the advertisement, which claimed "Thirst Knows No Boundaries."

In December 1941 he started training in Quebec, where he accumulated 66 hours in a Fleet Finch. After 223 hours he completed his flight training and shipped to an Operational Training Unit in England in October 1942 for advanced training. In January 1943 he had his first flight in a Hurricane. Thirteen days later, with head up and locked, he barely missed "pranging" his kite in a dead-stick landing because he neglected to switch fuel tanks and his engine quit. He was assigned to an operational unit, which proved boring. In order to overcome the boredom he became reckless. Buzzing low, he chopped six inches off his prop, and two days later he tore off his tail wheel.

As a Sergeant Pilot he managed to obtain a transfer to the U.S. Army Air Force, thereby becoming a Flight Officer training

in P-47s. His instructor was Squadron Leader George "Screwball" Beurling, who had 31 Germans to his credit flying out of Malta. Hofer undoubtedly picked up many questionable habits from him. The Kidd was soon assigned to the 4th Fighter Group, 334 Squadron, with its steam-heated brick buildings, napkin rings, waitresses, and batmen. There the Group missions, because of the longer range planes flown, generally were bomber escort missions.

Prior to this time the British had been flying relatively short-range fighter planes, such as the Hurricane and the Spitfire. This relegated them primarily to defensive "hell-for-leather dogfights" and short-range operations, such as convoy patrol, as they defended their "island," as well as short offensive thrusts to the mainland. The main offensive work was done by British bombers operating at night in order to avoid the *Luftwaffe* fighters.

With the advent of the day-bombing tactics of the USAAF, the mission of the longer range U.S. fighters became one of protecting their bombers from the Nazi fighters as they defended their vulnerable targets from these more accurate bombing attacks. The Fighter mission, under Colonel Blakeslee, became protect the bombers, and protect each other. A wingman was expected to stay with and protect his unit leader so he could attack the enemy and not fear an enemy attack from his rear. The unit leader, meantime, was to protect his wingman in the same manner. The concept assumed that the whole operation was strengthened by being a *team* effort. A few fighter pilots never made the mental transition to this type of mission, and those few, like Kidd Hofer, constantly disregarded orders and responsibility, disappearing to hunt alone whenever the opportunity arose. These lone wolf missions were not necessarily fearless; they were more inclined to be foolhardy. They could, however, be fruitful in building up a personal score if one happened to be lucky enough to survive. Meanwhile, the element partner was left to fend for himself.

Hofer was a good flyer, and his lone wolf tactics built up his personal score. Fortunately, he also was extremely lucky in escaping many dangerous situations, since he was insecure in his ability to fly instruments and his navigational skills left a great deal to be desired. His disregard of aerial discipline earned him many reprimands, but it was not confined entirely to the air. He was picked up in London by MPs for not wearing his rank insignia on his trench coat, at which time they discovered he was not even carrying his identification card.

The Kidd's first combat mission was what was to become a routine for him. He became separated from his element leader when they were attacked by *Luftwaffe* planes and he headed home alone. On the way he encountered a Jerry attacking a P-47. He was able, undetected, to come up behind the Hun and blast him, unfortunately too late to save the other P-47. With minor changes

in detail this sort of episode happened frequently, and soon Hofer was the first Flight Officer to become an "Ace," followed shortly by earning the DFC. On 22 April he was promoted to Second Lieutenant.

This did not have any effect on his behavior, however, as he managed to take a nurse for a ride in a P-51 sitting on his lap. Occasionally he took his dog "Duke" for a ride. He enjoyed pulling up alongside a strange aircraft over England and ducking down, leaving only Duke's head visible in the cockpit and letting it appear that a dog was flying his airplane.

This writer's first experience with Hofer was very exciting as well as thrilling. Returning from a routine escort mission, somehow, as usual, Hofer became detached from the Group. Being his wingman, I stuck with him like glue. We soon encountered a lone Me-109 and Hofer attacked. He peppered the 109, and in desperation the pilot bailed out. It was so close that Hofer almost hit him. Flying off to his left but very tight to Hofer, I passed close to the Kraut and observed him clearly as he hung in his chute, waving to us. He had on his dress uniform, with medals displayed as if he were going to a ball. I was totally impressed with his black shiny boots glistening in the sun; I glanced down at my own dirty GI boots and my grungy flight suit and thought "What a strange situation," but he was down, and we were still flying; obviously, dress does not necessarily make one a victor.

In due course 6 June found the 4th involved in protecting the beach-head as the invasion of the Continent began. The Kidd's luck held, as his flight of four P-51s was bounced by a superior group of 109s and three of the Mustangs were shot down, with only Kidd surviving. Within a few days, orders were given that all personnel were to have immunization shots in preparation for a secret mission. Hofer refused, as he hated shots. As punishment he was grounded, forbidden from entering the bar for two weeks, and forbidden to go on the secret mission. Finally he relented, had his shots, and became eligible to go on the mission, a bomber escort "Shuttle Flight to Russia, on to Italy, and home to Debden."

Because of the length of the first leg of this mission—7 ½ hours and the longest ever flown—orders stipulated that there were to be no attacks on *Luftwaffe* planes except to protect the bombers, and formation was to remain intact throughout. A brief combat ensued over the bombing target and, as usual, Hofer disappeared. When the Group arrived in Piryatin two fighters were missing; one that had been shot down and Hofer's. Hofer had gotten lost and, with only a few drops of gas left, had managed to land in an airfield near Kiev. There he was to remain for four days, as the suspicious Russians kept him in protective custody while they checked his identity before sending him to rendezvous with the rest of his group.

This was only the first of his mishaps on the mission. He flew back to his original destination only to find that the Group had left on the second leg of the mission to Italy. Three planes remained with engine problems. When they became airworthy the four left for Italy. Two hours into their flight one pilot suggested to Hofer that he had the wrong heading. However, Hofer remained adamant, so the two others left to pursue a different course. One arrived in Italy at the destined base and one landed in Sicily. Hofer, running out of gas, followed a flight of British planes and landed in Malta, hundreds of miles off course. Five days later he rejoined his group.

The next day (2 July) the 4th joined fighters from the 15th Air Force to escort bombers on a raid to Budapest, Hungary. A group of 109s came up in force, and Ralph's element leader, having difficulty with his engine, was shot down; Hofer then went off alone and was never seen again.

Assuming that Ralph had been shot down, there ensued many stories as to who was responsible for the kill. Hofer was such a high-scoring icon that any German pilot would have been proud to have credit for his destruction. Research soon proved that two of the major claimants' stories were dismissed as false. It then became possible that he had been shot down by a young Hungarian pilot, but unfortunately, before the investigation could be completed, this pilot was killed. In any event, Hofer's plane had crashed with his body in it, and he was buried in Mostar, Yugoslavia, about three hundred miles from where his Group had engaged in fighting the *Luftwaffe*. Years later, investigation discovered that the most likely cause of the Kidd's demise was a flak battery, and that in his final act he rammed the battery as he went down, killing some of the gunners.

The mystery of Hofer and his life did not end with his death, however. A young woman wrote the Squadron Commander and claimed his personal items, saying she was his wife and the mother of his young daughter. Hofer's mother, on the other hand, tried unsuccessfully to claim his belongings, insisting the marriage to the woman was headed for divorce, had he survived.

What we know is that Hofer flew 74 missions with the 4th and scored 30 ½ e/a destroyed. He was awarded the Distinguished Flying Cross with three OLC, the Air Medal with one OLC, and the Purple Heart.

It was a pleasure to know him and to fly with him; it was always exciting. However, I would much rather be his Wingman than depend on him to be mine.

Captain **DAVID W. HOWE**

Howe was a Pennsylvanian from East Hickory, born on 6 February 1919. He joined the Royal Canadian Air Force in 1941 in Toronto, Canada, and earned his wings as a Sergeant Pilot on 8 October 1942.

David transferred to the United States Army Air Force on 3 June 1943, and was assigned to the 4th Fighter Group, 334 Squadron, in September.

Flying a P-47 Thunderbolt, he downed his first enemy aircraft, an FW-190, in February 1944. In March, flying a P-51, he downed two more *Luftwaffe* planes, and on 19 May, with additional victories, he became an Ace.

In April 1945, as a Captain, he returned to the States. He was the first pilot in the 8th Fighter Command to complete two combat tours without an abort, a total of 502 combat hours.

He left the service in August 1945 having 8 ½ enemy aircraft to his credit. He obtained a civilian commercial pilot rating and later became a test pilot with Bell Aircraft. He flew eight types of jets, including two VTOL (Vertical Takeoff and Landing) types.

He retired in 1981 and died of a massive stroke in May 1995, in Erie, Pennsylvania. He had earned the Distinguished Flying Cross with three Oak Leaf Clusters and the Air Medal with 13 Oak Leaf Clusters.

Captain **JOSEPH L. LANG**

Joe was born in Boston, Massachusetts, on 27 June 1922. He took his pilot training in the Royal Canadian Air Force and engaged in combat with the British Royal Air Force prior to transferring to the 4th Fighter Group, 334 Squadron on 28 December 1943. On 19 May he was credited with his first victory when he destroyed an Me-109 and a flying boat near Wismar, Germany. He became an Ace on 21 June near Warsaw, Poland, on the first leg of the shuttle-run to Russia. He shot down one of a group of 20-plus Me-109s attacking the bombers after they dropped their bombs on Lezno, Poland.

He was promoted to Captain, but Lang met his fate over Manheim after downing 2 Me-109s on 14 October 1944. His final transmission, picked up by his separated Wingman, was, "This is Lang. I'm down below the clouds with 10 Me-109s. I got two. I don't know where I am and I need help." Apparently the 109s were able to down him before help could arrive. His remains were removed from the burning wreckage of his plane.

Joe was credited with 11.8 enemy aircraft destroyed and was awarded the Distinguished Flying Cross with three Oak Leaf Clusters and the Air Medal with 3 Oak Leaf Clusters.

Captain **DONALD M. MALMSTEN**

Donald Malmsten enlisted in the Army Air Corps from Burell, Nebraska. I first met Don at Dale Mabry Field near Tallahasee, FL, where we had been assigned to train in P-51s prior to shipping to England. He and I and our wives became good friends. During the course of our training Don and I were assigned to go up and practice camera gunnery. Accordingly, we met and arranged that I would be the target for the first encounter. I then started to fly straight and level while Don came up behind me to take a camera synchronization shot. This was a normal routine to see that the guns and the camera were zeroed in on the same target.

All of a sudden my plane started to shudder violently and the engine began to vibrate. I broke off immediately and headed for our field, thinking that Malmsten had overshot and started to chew the tail of my plane with his prop. Upon landing, we discovered that Don had inadvertently turned the gun switch to "Guns and Camera" instead of "Camera." Unfortunately, his kite had been on a gunnery mission the day before and the armorer had not removed the unused ammunition.

The result of these two errors was that, as far as I can ascertain, I am the only fighter pilot to ever be shot down over Florida! In turn, Malmsten was probably the first Allied fighter pilot to claim a victory over Florida. Unfortunately, the "Upper Echelon" did not see the humor in this incident. The armorer was busted to private and Don was considered for punishment. Since it was to be only another day or two prior to our transfer to the Port of Embarkation, the need for fighter pilots was more urgent than the need to make an example. Don was let off the hook with the proviso that he be accompanied 24 hours a day by an MP to keep him from partaking of alcoholic beverages until he shipped out. This was not necessarily to Don's liking, but was certainly better than any alternative prospects.

Our training completed, Don and several of us classmates shipped out to England. We completed our overseas training at Goxhill. Don and I both ended up in the 4th Fighter Group, 334 Squadron. He was an aggressive pilot and loved to strafe trucks, trains, and military convoys, as well as dogfight with *Luftwaffe* planes. On August 1944 Malmsten was leading Green Section on a strafing mission southeast of Paris to destroy locomotives and boxcars believed to contain buzz-bombs. Near Dijon, his Section clobbered a couple of locomotives and received some intense flak. He became separated from his wingman but continued alone, blowing up three more when he came upon some trucks. He clobbered one and, pulling up, noticed his engine had started to smoke. He was very low and could only keep it running for a couple of minutes before it caught fire.

He crash landed in a beet field and got out of the flaming plane. Discarding his equipment, he took off across the fields for about a mile and crawled into a ditch filled with weeds. Here he discovered that he had burns on his cheek and nose. He walked at night and for three days before being picked up by the Underground. They introduced him to the Maquis, who cared for him for a pleasant four weeks until he could be smuggled out and returned to London in September, and thence back to his Squadron.

Since I had been introduced to flak and had become a POW, I next saw Don back in the States at Dover Air Force Base after VE-Day, when Don got notice of his discharge. We and our wives were quietly celebrating, playing bridge and drinking in our motel room. Don, in his exuberance, proceeded to get stinking drunk, unable to continue the game. The next day they left for Nebraska, where he had a ranch.

I never heard from him again, but I did hear that he had a habit of flying his plane into the nearest town for Friday night relaxation and flying home afterwards with very little "bottle to throttle" time. It appears he had flown his plane into a mountain one night and was killed.

Donald Malmsten had 10.5 enemy aircraft to his credit and had earned the Purple Heart, the Distinguished Flying Cross, and the Air Medal with ten Oak Leaf Clusters.

Captain **JACK D. McFADDEN**

From Brookville, PA, Captain McFadden was assigned to the 4th Fighter Group, 334 Squadron 11 June 1944, where he remained until the end of the war. He became "A" Flight Commanding Officer in March 1945.

Captain McFadden had five enemy aircraft destroyed and was awarded the Air Medal with ten Oak Leaf Clusters.

Major **MICHAEL G. McPHARLIN**

Michael McPharlin, known as Mike or "Wee Mike," was a Pilot Officer in No. 71 Eagle Squadron, a group of American pilots fighting the Nazis under British command. He had joined the Royal Canadian Air Force from Hastings, Michigan, and after completing his flying training he transferred into the British Royal Air Force. He named his plane "Wee Ginny." He made many close friends in the Eagle Squadron, but when his friends transferred to the newly-commissioned U.S. 4th Fighter Group, 334 Squadron, he did not, but was instead assigned to the 339 Fighter Group. Nevertheless, he maintained an ongoing friendship with the 334th and was frequently loaned to and flew on missions with his 334th buddies.

On 19 August 1942 he had to bail out over Dieppe, but fortunately was returned to his Squadron. On 6 June 1944, flying with his friends of 334 Squadron, he was not so lucky. He reported to White Leader that his left magneto was out and he was heading for home nursing his rough engine. He was never heard from again! He had destroyed 6.5 German planes.

Captain **NICHOLAS MEGURA**

On his third trip to Berlin, flying his P-51 "Ill Wind," Cowboy, as he was known, contemplated two previous trips over Germany where he had scored double enemy aircraft destroyed. As the Mustangs approached rendezvous with the bombers five Me-109s dove down at them from out of the sun. Megura latched on to one of them, which he quickly dispatched, and immediately had to break away with another one on his tail. He evaded and went to the rescue of a straggler Fort under attack by several 109s. He zeroed in on one and the Hun reluctantly bailed out as his plane belched smoke.

He then fell in behind a 109 which was circling in the landing pattern of an airfield. No one seemed to notice him as he was about to shoot the 109 with its wheels and flaps down. However, he was suddenly recognized and attacked head-on by three 109s, who obviously were not happy with this intrusion. He avoided them and fired at the landing 109, damaging it as it hit the runway. He outdistanced his pursuers and headed for Debden.

He soon encountered a JU-88 which he fired on with only one gun operative, knocking out one of its engines before he ran out of ammunition. He returned to Debden having scored another double destroyed and two others damaged. A month later he was awarded the Distinguished Service Cross for this and the two previous actions.

This was not an unusual day for Megura, who lived a life of aggressiveness and audacity. He came from Ansonia, Connecticut, born on 28 July 1920. As a freshman at Philips University, he did not see eye-to-eye with the President on a matter of discipline for some freshman highjinks and was promptly expelled. He obtained some money from his parents and, along with a friend, purchased a Model "A" and proceeded to tour the States. After visiting 46 of them he returned and acquired a motorcycle. Due to his mother's insistence, he soon divested himself of this "dangerous thing" and went to work at the Vought-Sikorski plant, taking up flying on the side. He joined the RCAF and, when the opportunity arose, he transferred to the U.S. Army Air Force in July 1943. He was assigned to the 4th Fighter Group, 334 Squadron. Nine months later, having flown P-47s and then P-51s, he had destroyed 16 enemy aircraft and damaged six, 15 of them destroyed in a two-month period.

His combat career ended 23 May. The Group intercepted 30 plus enemy aircraft which were also engaged by several P-38s. Cowboy, while attacking three Me-109s, had his fuselage raked by gunfire from a P-38 that mistook him for a 109. His coolant system was violated, causing him to consider bailing out. However, he could not open his canopy and began nursing his stricken plane toward Denmark. He then daringly kept nursing it farther toward Sweden, where he bellied in at Kalmar Airdrome and was immediately interned.

On 28 June he arrived back at Debden, but due to diplomatic relations he was no longer permitted to fly combat. Aggressive and unafraid to attack superior numbers, he had already made his mark in combat, but was assigned to strictly administrative duties.

Megura continued in the Air Force, retiring as a Lieutenant Colonel. He died 4 November 1988. He had been awarded the Distinguished Service Cross, the Distinguished Flying Cross with five Oak Leaf Clusters, the Purple Heart, and the Air Medal with three Oak Leaf Clusters.

Major **HENRY L. MILLS**

Major Mills (better known as Hank) was born in New York City 18 October 1917. His various civilian accomplishments were playing varsity football while attending Dartmouth College and earning a Bachelors of Arts degree, as well as graduating in 1939. He then went to join the Royal Canadian Air Force in Canada upon the outbreak of war in Europe.

Upon earning his wings as a pilot officer he was posted to No.71 (Eagle Squadron). In October 1942 he transferred to the United States Army Air Force and was assigned to the 4th Fighter Group, 334 Squadron.

His first kills were two FW-190s on 16 August 1943 while flying a P-47 Thunderbolt. In October he was appointed Squadron Operations Officer. In February 1944 he became an ace and was soon promoted to Major. On 6 March he downed his last enemy aircraft, a FW-190, and minutes later, on the same mission, he was shot down; his engine failed, and he had to bail out immediately, becoming a Prisoner of War.

He escaped from his captors in Stalag Luft III in March 1945 and returned to England. He was discharged in 1946. Upon his return to life as a civilian he established Mills, Talbot, and Company, dealing with electrical manufactures in New York and New England, and retiring in 1987.

Hank had flown Spitfires, Thunderbolts, and Mustangs and had destroyed six enemy aircraft. He was awarded the Distinguished Flying Cross with three Oak Leaf Clusters, the Air Medal with three Oak Leaf Clusters, and the Purple Heart.

Major **GERALD MONTGOMERY**

Major Montgomery was a native of Dallas, Texas, when he entered the Air Corps. After acquiring his wings he was assigned to the 4th Fighter Group, 334 Squadron on 15 May 1943. He remained in that Squadron until the end of the war. At the end of his first tour he earned a leave to the States, having destroyed 11 enemy aircraft. His first plane, a Thunderbolt, was named Texas. Upon return from his leave he was assigned a Mustang, which he promptly named "Sizzlin Liz." He soon was named Squadron Operations Officer. He continued to knock out enemy aircraft and eventually had 14.5 to his credit when the war ended.

By the end of January 1944 334 Squadron had destroyed 48 enemy aircraft. A pool of 30 Pounds was collected from the pilots, to be paid to the one who destroyed the 50th plane for the Squadron.

On 10 February a support mission was flown to Brunswick, Germany.

An aggressive Group of Me-109s and Fw-190s attacked and were engaged by the Group. Three pilots from 334 Squadron (Lt Thomas Biel, Major Gerald Montgomery, and Captain Victor France) each scored one enemy aircraft shot down with no way of determining which one got the 50th. To resolve the situation each of the three received 10 Pounds.

Two months later Lt. Biel was shot down and killed. In March Captain France, while chasing a 109, hit the ground; his plane exploded and he was killed. Major Montgomery was the only one of the three to have survived the war. He is believed to have been killed in action in the Korean War. He was carried as MIA until May 2004, when a marker was placed in Arlington Cemetery with full military honors and a fly-by.

He had been awarded the Distinguished Flying Cross with four OLCs, the Air Medal with 15 OLCs, and the Campaign Medal with 6 Battle Stars.

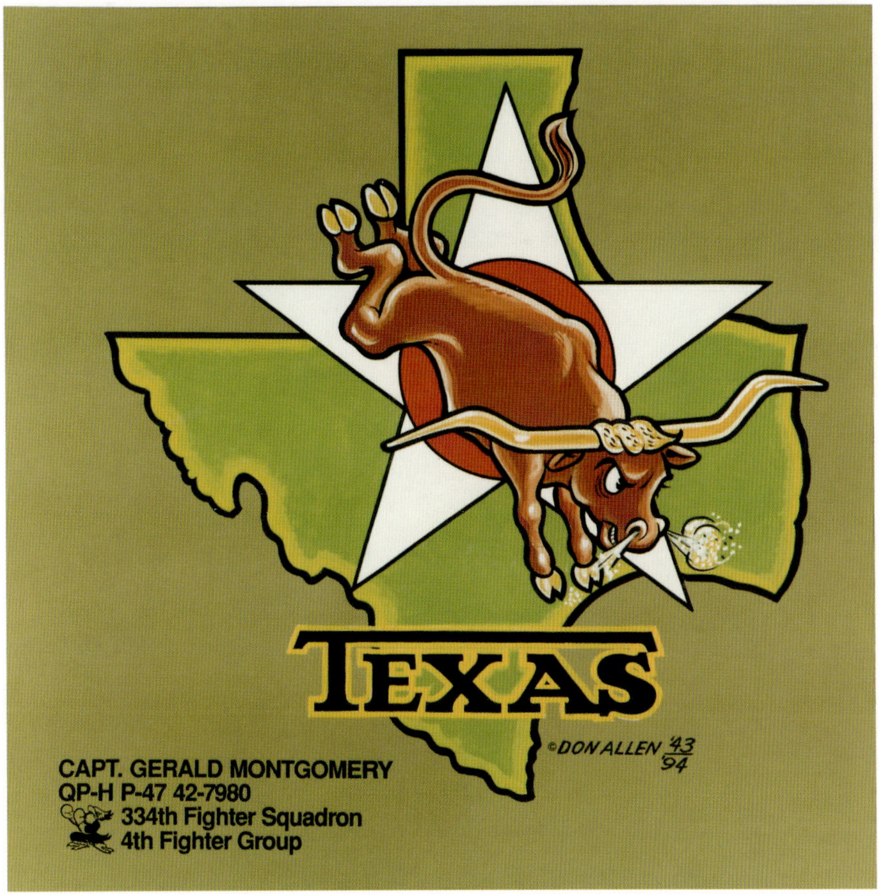
TEXAS
©DON ALLEN '43 '94
CAPT. GERALD MONTGOMERY
QP-H P-47 42-7980
334th Fighter Squadron
4th Fighter Group

SIZZLIN LIZ
QP H

Lt. Colonel **LOUIS H. NORLEY**

Louis Norley was from Conrad, Montana. He was assigned to the 4th Fighter Group, 336 Squadron, on 10 July 1943. It did not take him long to acquire the nickname "Red Dog," not because of his red hair, but for his propensity to lose money playing Red Dog poker. He was very intelligent and a great flyer, but rarely drew attention to his achievements. The total of 16.3 aircraft destroyed is an indication of his flying and gunnery ability. His desire to fight the Huns was such that on 3 March, when the first daylight raid by U.S. bombers was to be escorted by the 4th, he opted to go on the raid rather than take his scheduled pass to London.

From May 1944 to the middle of August he was on leave in the U.S., having finished his first tour. On 30 August he was named CO of 335 Squadron. He still roomed with Fred Glover, who was Squadron Commander of 336 Squadron. They had many name calling arguments over who shot down what as their friendly rivalry took on an intense character. On 2 November Norley shot down an Me-163 rocket-powered fighter the first time he had occasion to use the new K-14 gunsight. He became very positive about this new equipment.

On 25 January Red Dog was assigned to 334 Squadron as C.O. On 31 March he started his third tour with 554 combat hours to his credit. He had acquired the Distinguished Flying Cross and the Air Medal with 13 OLCs. The war was soon over, and he then did a tour in the Korean War, eventually retiring as a Lt. Colonel. He died in Oakland, California, 1 August 1967.

Colonel **STEVE N. (SPIRO) PISANOS**

Steve was born in Athens, Greece, son of a subway driver, in November 1919. At the age of 12 he saw a Greek Air Force plane performing aerobatics and, as the biplane flew away, Steve, totally captivated, knew that he must become an aviator; nothing else would be acceptable. School and books meant nothing to him until at age 18 he discovered he had insufficient academic qualifications to enter the Greek Air Force Academy. Undaunted, he made up his mind to go to America, where he understood he could get an excellent education free and learn to fly.

Getting to America was beset with obstacles: he didn't speak English; he had no money; and he knew no one in America to help him. He tried to stow away on a luxury liner, but he was caught. Through a friend, he met a Merchant Marine sailor and was able to join the Greek Merchant Marine. He soon found himself on a freighter with a destination of Baltimore. While the ship was awaiting a berth in the harbor of Baltimore he managed to jump ship and buy a train ticket to New York. In New York, by sheer luck, he ran into a couple of men who were speaking Greek. Three days later he started working in a bakery owned by a Greek family. His long hours kept Steve from learning English by attending night school so he obtained a Greek/English dictionary and taught himself the American language.

About seven months after his arrival in the U.S. he had mastered enough English to take up flying lessons. Almost every dollar he made went for flying lessons, and he earned a private pilot's license from the Civil Aeronautics Authority. Meanwhile, the war in Europe was in full swing, so he tried to join the U.S. Army but was turned down because he wasn't a citizen.

Desperate to get into the war, and with 170 flying hours, he contacted the Clayton-Knight Committee and joined the British RAF. Training in England as a fighter pilot, he graduated as a Pilot Officer and was assigned to the 268th Fighter Squadron.

Meanwhile, the Greek Air Force, in exile, was searching for Greek pilots who had escaped Greece before the Nazis conquered their country with the thought of impressing them into the Greek Air Force, which was organizing a Spitfire squadron in Egypt. Steve did not want to go to Egypt. In order to retain Steve, Chesley Peterson had him transferred into the No. 71 Eagle Squadron of American volunteers. In September 1942 the Eagle Squadrons were absorbed into the U.S. Army Air Force, including Steve and the others in No. 71 Eagle Squadron, even though he was not a U.S. citizen. In May 1943, through the efforts of Col. Peterson, a close friend of the Ambassador, Steve was naturalized in London. He thus became the first person in American history to become a U.S. citizen on foreign soil. Steve recalls this as the happiest day of his life. That night the sign at the bar in Debden read "Tonight all drinks are on Steve Pisanos, American."

On a mission 5 March 1943, fifty feet into the air and wheels up on takeoff, his Spitfire's engine lost power. He crashed and nosed over when his wheels buckled. One crash was not enough, however; while being towed to the hangar the cart on which the Spitfire was being towed broke down and the plane again crashed to the ground.

On 5 March 1944, after more than 100 combat missions in Spitfires, P-47s, and a P-51 Mustang named "Miss Plainfield," and the destruction of 10 German aircraft in the air, Steve's luck ran out. His engine quit on an escort mission over France and he was forced to crash land. He decided to bail out at 2000 feet. He trimmed the aircraft to fly on its own, released the canopy, and tried to stand up and step out on the left wing, but was hung up by something in the cockpit. He saw that the plug at the end of his nylon dinghy cord was caught somewhere underneath the seat. His effort to loosen it was unsuccessful, so he reached for his escape knife by his right boot, but it was not there. He sat down and worked the cord left and right, finally loosening it. Now free, he stood up and stepped out on the wing. Just as he was about to slide down the wing he saw he was too close to the ground to bail out, and he saw that the powerless plane was headed for the roof of a barn in the clearing where he was planning to land. Fearing that he would hit the barn, and with no time left, he reached into the cockpit and pulled back on the stick, barely missing the roof. Passing the barn, his right wingtip hit the soft ground and the plane skidded along with Steve on his knees on the wing hanging on desperately. The plane stopped suddenly and Steve was hurled through the air, barely missing the stopped propeller blades, and landed thirty feet away.

When he regained consciousness severe pain made him think he had lost his left arm, but he soon discovered it was still attached to his body. In spite of the intense pain, he crawled back to his plane to set it on fire. He dragged his parachute and placed it in the cockpit. Then he took off his silk scarf, dipped it into the wing tank to soak it with gas, and while searching for a match in his escape kit, he became aware of soldiers running toward him, shooting as they ran. With no time to finish the job he scrambled down from the wing and ran full bore into the nearby wood. By doubling back in the wood he eluded the soldiers and spent the next five days distancing himself from the scene. Living on grass and dandelions and sleeping under bridges, he finally made contact with the French Resistance. They verified his identity, hid him, and arranged medical treatment for his shoulder, which had been dislocated.

He soon became involved in sabotage with his French comrades. After six months working with the Resistance in Paris, Steve was able to escape from the Nazi occupied territory and make his way back to England. He immediately wanted to return to combat, but his knowledge of the Underground made it too risky for his French Compatriots and he was sent back to the States.

Steve was assigned to Wright Field as a test pilot. He tested both prop planes and jets, including Me-109s, FW-190s, and Me-262s. He later tested the new Lockheed P-80 Shooting Star at Muroc Lake, California. Unable to get a regular commission due to his lack of a college degree, in 1946 he left the service and went with TWA as a First Officer. He was recalled to active duty in 1948 and served at the Pentagon. While there he started to attend college at the University of Maryland for a degree. He later was assigned for a tour with NATO.

He flew 375 combat missions in Vietnam while commanding an airlift squadron. Steve was promoted to the rank of Colonel and made Deputy Commander of a SAC ICBM Wing.

In spite of all his adventures, Steve regards his most interesting assignment as when he was on the U.S. Mission for aid to Greece His primary job was fighting competition with the French and the British for the arming of Greece with modern jet fighters for their Air Force. He eventually succeeded in the sale of two Squadrons of F-4s, including spares and training worth 300 million dollars for the U.S.

In 1973, with 30 years of distinguished service and 7,000 hours of flying in over 50 types of planes, he retired from the Air Force as a Colonel. He had earned a B.S. at the University of Maryland, and attended the Air Command and Staff College and the Air War College. He had shot down 10 enemy aircraft, and received over 25 decorations from four different countries. Among his awards were the Legion of Merit with two Oak Leaf Clusters, the Distinguished Flying Cross with four Oak Leaf Clusters, the Purple Heart, the British Star, the French *Croix de Guerre* / Silver Star, and the Vietnamese Medal of Honor, 1st class.

I have known Steve long enough to know his knowledge of English never leaves him at a loss for words. This distinguished aviator has put his language skills to work in his recently published book of his memoirs called *The Flying Greek*, on sale at book stores nationwide.

Captain **CARL G. PAYNE**

Captain Payne was from San Antonio, TX, and was assigned to the 4th Fighter Group, 334 Squadron 22 September 1944, where he remained until 21 September 1945. He was appointed Squadron Operations Officer in July 1945 prior to being assigned to the 4th Mobile R and R Section.

Payne had 5 1/2 enemy aircraft to his credit and was awarded the Air Medal with five Oak Leaf Clusters.

Captain **ALEXANDER RAFALOVICH**

Alex was from San Pedro, California. He was assigned to the 4th Fighter Group, 334th Fighter Squadron in February 1943 while they were still flying Spitfires. As they were transitioning to P-47s the Squadron was off operations for 45 days, so Alex took a short leave and got married, returning 18 March.

Routine combat followed in the P-47s until Group Commander Don Blakeslee insisted and was given the opportunity to trade the P-47s for the new long-range P-51s. The pilots were delighted with the new craft in spite of the fact that it was more vulnerable to damage since the engine was liquid-cooled. The transition was made with most of the pilots having little more than a few hours flight time to familiarize themselves with the 51s prior to flying them into combat.

On 21 March 1944 the 4th. had no scheduled mission, and so initiated a rhubarb to France, led by Colonel Jim Clark. As 334 Squadron attacked an airfield in the Bordeaux area, Alex and his wingman were clobbering a Do-217 which was trying to land, and as they were pulling up, they were bounced unexpectedly by a flight of Fw-190s. Alex suddenly discovered his oil pressure was going down to zero. As he climbed up to 3,000 feet his glycol coolant was streaming out of his exhaust, so he immediately bailed out.

He speculated that since he did not feel any hits to his plane, as he was approaching the airfield he was so low he probably hit the top of a tree, damaging his scoop and the oil cooler plumbing inside it.

Faced with immediate action, thoughts raced through his mind. He later wrote:

"The procedures run through your mind all of the time so you train yourself mentally. You're like a robot. You just snap the canopy open and you bail out, you don't think because there is only one option and that is to get out. It's one, two, three, and out you go. You don't think; you react. If you start thinking, it's too late."

The parachute ride was fast:

"Before I knew it, I was on the ground. I will never forget the tail of the plane flying underneath me. I had my legs spread and saw the tail of the plane pass right under me. After I landed I hid my chute and started walking. I met a few Frenchmen and showed them a little I.D. card. They thanked me and kept going.

"Just before dark I went to a woman's house. She had three kids and she took me in that night. The next morning she gave me civilian clothes, led me to the railroad station, and bought me a ticket. I was in a military zone that the Germans had. I wasn't in the middle of France, I was on the coast. I found a map of the railroad system and just hopped from one station to the other. No one asked me any questions. I got all the way down to the Pyrenees and then some Frenchman turned me in. It might have been for the reward or for the fact that if the Germans caught anyone helping the Allies it was a very serious crime. Frenchmen are OK, they just fought a lousy war, that's all."

Alex spent the rest of the war as a POW. He had five planes destroyed to his credit and had earned the Distinguished Flying Cross with one Oak Leaf Cluster, the Air Medal with one Oak Leaf Cluster, and the POW Medal. He retired in California.

Lt **GROVER C. SIEMS,** JR.

Lt. Grover C. Siems, Jr., was from Montagh, Long Island, NY. After graduating from high school he worked at the Ranger Airplane Plant in Farmingdale, NY. He craved action, and soon joined the U.S. Army Air Corps as an Aviation Cadet. He graduated as a Fighter Pilot in October 1943 at Moore Field, Mission, Texas. His exposure to combat aircraft was limited to 10 hours in aging P-40s. After graduation he was transferred to Dale Mabry Field, Florida, where he received flight training in P-51s prior to being shipped to England.

At Gaux Hill, England, he received combat training in P-51s; and then, with several of his classmates, he was assigned to the 4th Fighter Group at Debden as a replacement pilot under Col. Donald Blakeslee. Grover, a master at one-upmanship, was soon sporting a pair of non-issue, high British flight boots, so as to appear an old hand in the Group.

The 4th was an aggressive Group, originally made up of the British Eagle Squadrons, and had just been switched from P-47s to P-51s. Missions were hot and heavy, as their long range P-51s were called on to escort bombers ever farther into Germany. By 5 May 1944 Grover had destroyed his fifth enemy aircraft to become an Ace. By the end of May several of his classmates were already missing in action or prisoners of war.

On 6 June, at 2:30 AM, the Group took off in drizzling rain and headed for the invasion front. Grover was assigned to fly cover for a battleship shelling inland targets in support of the invasion troops. He was able to see the ship fire salvos and see the rounds hit their target and explode 15 to 20 miles inland. Later that day, on mission number three, he shot down an Me-109, but crossing near Paris, he received a hit on the right side of his engine, causing it to lose power. By using full-rich fuel mixture he managed to coax it across the Channel and make a dead-stick, wheels-down landing in a coastal pasture.

On 21 June, after several weather delays, the Group took off on its historic shuttle-flight to Russia. They had been briefed on what baggage they must take and how the mission was to be accomplished. They were required to take a set of class "A"s, toilet paper, and soap. They were to escort bombers which were crewed primarily with 4th Group maintenance personnel as gunners, who were to maintain the 51s during their stay in Russia.

The size of the armada of bombers and fighters indicated a possible major attack on Frankfurt, and the Germans put up a wall of smoke and flak in response. A close burst killed Grover's engine and he prepared to bail out, but he managed to restart the engine and continue with the Group. Shortly thereafter they encountered an impressive formation of yellow-nosed Me-109s. However, the Germans, outnumbered ten to one, decided not to attack.

After seven and a half hours they landed on a grass field in Piryatin lit by a Fourth of July shower of varied colored flares.

They exchanged greetings and then sacked out in their sleeping bags. Shortly, all hell broke loose as antiaircraft fire and flares lit up the camp. Siems' sleeping bag zipper jammed and he had to do a fast sack race to get to the crowded slit trench.

The next day they took off for Chuquiev, about 200 miles away, for safety from German attack. They found sleeping quarters in a former hospital. The "beds" were straw covered platforms about 80 feet long along the walls where they slept side-by-side, with a 40' by 10' outdoor latrine for their "convenience."

They were invited to a banquet of raw fish and donkey stew with an unending supply of vodka for the many toasts that ensued. The toasts "To Stalin," "To Churchill," and "To Roosevelt" were drunk with water glasses filled with vodka and always "bottoms up." By midnight everyone was stoned and grateful for the straw mattresses.

The next morning started with a straight razor shave done by a huge muscular man dressed only in pants. Then the party started again with music from an accordion and a trumpet, and both musicians were excellent. Soldiers of both sexes danced and drank for hours without tiring.

One of the pilots had taxied into a slit trench and was mired beyond hope. There was no heavy equipment in the camp, and it seemed that the plane would be lost. A Russian officer said that at 8 AM the next day he would recover the plane. Promptly at 8 AM 60 Russian soldiers appeared, stationed themselves under the plane, sang a rhythmic song and, at a word, they lifted the plane and placed it on firm ground.

On the 26th the Group took off for Italy on the next leg of their odyssey. In Italy there were a couple of days' free time for swimming and rest. Grover, in his typical unorthodox manner, managed to trade his issue '45 caliber pistol to some huckster for a Navy '38 which caught his eye; later it malfunctioned in spite of its eye appeal.

Then, on 2 July, Col. Blakeslee led the 4th on a bomber escort mission to Budapest, Hungary. They encountered a formation of 75 to 80 aggressive Me-109s. Siems was flying at Deacon Hively's wing as Hively shot down a '109 and in turn received fire, losing his canopy and loosening his eyeball from its socket. Grover shot the Hun off Deacon's tail, but in turn was severely wounded by a canon shell exploding in his cockpit. He immediately headed back to Foggia, Italy. Weak from loss of blood, he landed but was unable to get out of the cockpit. Receiving no attention, he managed to kick on his gun switch and send a volley over the control tower. This precipitated immediate action, and he was hauled off to the hospital, where he was pronounced dead and sent to the morgue.

Paralyzed, but very much alive, he managed to move a finger which moved the sheet covering his body. An orderly, seeing the movement, rushed him back to the hospital, where they immediately gave him transfusions and "brought him back to life." When he became conscious he discovered they had awarded him the Purple Heart—posthumously.

That was not the end of his troubles, however. When he recovered considerably he was presented with a statement of charges for $55,000 for his plane, which had disappeared. Fortunately, Grover had made friends with a pilot while in the hospital who had access to a C-47, and they set out to search for his plane.

Within two hours they found it. A Colonel from 15th AF HQ had adopted it for his own. Since he had not repainted it, it was easy to spot from the air—invasion stripes and a red nose—there was not another one like it in the theatre. The Colonel signed off with no argument, and Grover was off the hook.

In September Grover was taken off the 4th's roster and returned to the States, where he was discharged. Several years later I met him at an air show, shortly before he died the *second time* from a burst aneurism. He had 7.8 planes to his credit and had earned the Silver Star, the Distinguished Flying Cross with Oak Leaf Cluster, the Air Medal with three Oak Leaf Clusters, and the Purple Heart.

Captain **WILLIAM B. SMITH**

Captain Smith was from Bluefield, Virginia. He was attached to the 4th Fighter Group, 334 Squadron on 23 May 1943. He downed various enemy aircraft one at a time over a period of several months. He completed a tour, returning to the States on leave 2 June 1944. Returning to combat 17 August on his second tour, he downed another enemy aircraft. On 13 September, while strafing an airdrome near Ulm, Germany, his engine was hit by flak. He was able to pull up to 400 feet, but rolled over and dove into the ground, exploding upon impact.

He had destroyed 7 ¼ enemy aircraft and was awarded the Distinguished Flying Cross with one Oak Leaf Cluster and the Air Medal with seven Oak Leaf Clusters.

Major **WINSLOW M. SOBANSKI** (Mike)

Sobanski was born in New York City on 29 July 1919 while his mother was visiting her sister on vacation from her home in Poland. She also visited her close friends Harry Bruno and his wife Nydia. Harry had been a WWI Royal Canadian Air Force pilot and was a public relations consultant. Shortly after Mike was born he and his mother returned to Poland, where Mike received his education. He was a university student when the Germans invaded Poland in 1939. He attempted to join the Polish Air Force, but it was soon annihilated by Hitler's modern *Luftwaffe*. He then became an infantryman and headed towards the front on a troop train.

The train was bombed, and Mike was pinned in the wreckage, suffering three broken ribs. He was extricated and put on a train for transport to a hospital. Hardly able to breathe because of his injuries, and with no food, he lay in a filthy boxcar for five days before arriving at an old monastery which was being used as a hospital. He then waited two days before they could treat him. Finally they put a cast on him, but the Germans were advancing and Mike and others tried to escape but were captured and moved to a hospital in an old Russian fort surrounded by a moat.

Mike, believed to be immobile, was left unguarded. At night he left the hospital, waded through the moat, and hitchhiked and walked 200 miles to Warsaw, where he found his home in ruins and the city occupied by the Nazis. He found his father, a former Polish infantry colonel, now suffering from total depression because of his country's defeat.

By means of his American citizenship Mike obtained a visa and was permitted to leave. He walked and hitchhiked circuitously out of German-occupied territory and took a berth as a seaman aboard an Italian ship. The ship made its way to the U.S., and when it docked in Baltimore, Mike jumped ship and made his way to New York City, where he looked up his relatives. They introduced him to their family friend, Harry Bruno, now a recruiter for the Royal Canadian Air Force. Harry arranged for him to join and be accepted in the RCAF as a pilot trainee.

He soon washed out of the training program because of his inability to speak English. Harry Bruno intervened and Mike was reinstated while continuing to learn English. He finally earned his wings in October 1941. He boarded a ship on 3 November and headed for Scotland. He was delighted to find himself in training as a fighter pilot in Miles Masters and Hurricanes. He then joined 416 Squadron RCAF, where he met his future friend James Goodson, and they both eventually joined the Eagle Squadron and finally transferred into the 4th Fighter Group. Meanwhile, Mike got to fly Spitfires on convoy patrol, which he found very boring. On 22 September 1942 he was discharged from the RAF and posted to No.133 Eagle Squadron as a Second Lieutenant, and on the 29th he and Jim transferred to the 4th Fighter Group, 334 Squadron. There they were assigned as roommates, and they soon became great friends.

Mike found the 4th to be what he wanted. He had the desired opportunity to fight and kill Germans. He had a particular driving hatred because of what they had done to him, to his home, and to

his Poland. Mike was a strict taskmaster, and drilled his squadron with a firm hand. On days with no combat he led Balbos. These were low level formation practice missions. With Mike they never became easier or less dangerous. I remember one in particular; Mike was leading and I was flying his wing. It was a very low-level and tight formation exercise. He was really hugging the contours of the hills and valleys, and it took every bit of my skill to stay as tight on his wing as he wanted and still keep an eye on the area in front of me. Off to my left was another element of two facing the same sort of challenge. The radio was silent except for Mike's frequent "urgings" to close it up and keep your head moving. Suddenly, an unexpected voice broke in and said, "This is Red Four, would someone check my plane; it is flying rough, and the windscreen is covered with something?" A cursory check by the element leader indicated some damage to his wing and suggested that he return to base.

As Red Four came in to land his plane started to stall at a considerably higher speed than normal so he came in under power. Upon landing, an inspection indicated that the beautiful Mustang was no longer beautiful. The leading edge of both wings was crushed, in some places back to the main spar, utterly destroying the normal airfoil, which caused the plane to stall at a higher speed upon landing. The windscreen was covered with sap and bits of leafy material. Adding insult to injury, the air scoop contained a six-foot piece of tree trunk about ten to twelve inches in diameter. Obviously he had flown straight through an imposing tree and never even knew it. Apparently he had been so intent in watching his element leader that he was oblivious to what had been in front of him. That night he became exceedingly drunk and the next day he was gone. Obviously, Blakeslee meant it when he said, "You prang a plane unnecessarily and you will never fly with us again!"

In addition to Mike's zeal for destruction of the Nazis he found time to keep a diary, written in Polish, and a log book with very comprehensive records and notes, and was able to maintain a fair amount of social life. Both Polish and English women found him to be attractive and desirable. He also did many precise drawings and cartoons of various facets of his training. He was very proud of the Polish soldiers he met in England and enjoyed their company. They tried to get him to join a Polish squadron, but he thought of himself as an American and expected to go there to live after the war. Unfortunately he never got to return to the States, having been shot down and killed on D-Day. He was leading a section of four Mustangs strafing a truck convoy near Rouen when they were attacked by over fifteen Me-109s and Fw-190s. All four of his section were shot down and killed.

Upon Mike's death Jim Goodson took charge of Mike's effects, including his diary, his book of drawings, and his log book. He proposed to deliver these to Mike's girlfriend, Marishia, in Poland once the war was concluded. Eventually Jim made the trip to Poland, found Marishia, and met with her.

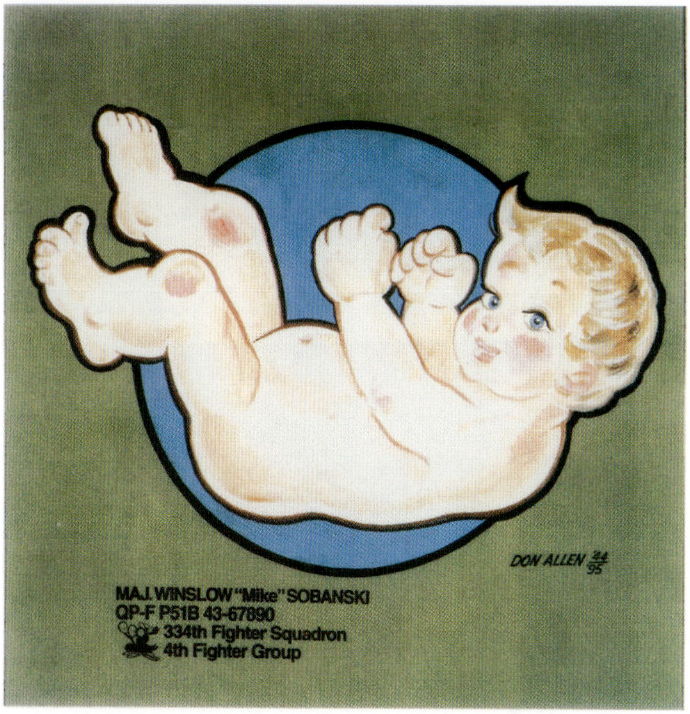

She was very apprehensive and would not accept Mike's belongings due to fear of the Soviets who now occupied Poland and might consider it to be subversive.

Jim next presented Mike's effects to his relatives in New York, who subsequently gave them to a museum. Years later a young collector, Jim Kirkup, who had a private museum, found them in the museum's basement, recognized their historic value, and acquired them for his display. Quite by chance, I visited his museum and was astounded to find this material accumulated by my former Squadron Commander. I was encouraged by the owner to copy it, have it translated into English, and use it as an important adjunct to a book I was writing about service in the 4th Group. I was delighted to have access to this rare find and used it in a biography of Mike's life in my previous book *One Down-One Dead*.

Mike had earned the Distinguished Flying Cross with an Oak Leaf Cluster and the Air Medal with two Oak Leaf Clusters, and had credit for six enemy aircraft destroyed. Although he was American by birth, he is considered to be a Polish hero for his contributions to the war effort in the service of Poland and in the service of the United States. His American citizenship allowed him the honor, which he would have desired, of being buried in the Ardennes American Cemetery in Neupre, Belgium.

1st Lieutenant **FRANK E. SPEER**

Frank was born on a cold day in January 1922 in Pittsburg, Pennsylvania. His father drove mules in a coal mine and his mother kept the books for the same mine. His father had health problems caused by the dampness in the mine, and when Frank was six the family moved to eastern Pennsylvania to a farm where the work environment was more conducive to his well being.

Frank grew up working on the farm, driving horses that pulled various farm implements in the fields, and milking cows morning and evening. On weekends and some nights he worked as a busboy in a local "Washington slept here" tavern. In the winter he worked on a hay-bailing crew, piling 150 pound bails for a few dollars a week. He was fortunate to have access to a private library stocked with hundreds of volumes, so when he was not working he was reading classics, and other books normally read by educated adults.

Out in the fields during the summer Frank frequently saw autogiros fly over from a nearby test field. That, plus a generous helping of comics like Buck Rogers and movie matinees of WWI dogfights, gave him an irresistible desire to fly. The desire became a must when a barnstorming pilot landed a Ford Tri-motor at a local dirt field, and Frank put down three dollars of his hard-earned savings for a ten minute ride in this corrugated monster of a plane.

Life went on. His avid reading made him an excellent student in a one-room grade school and later in high school. When he graduated, Frank became a lineman for the Bell Telephone Company; married (one month before Pearl Harbor); and toyed with the idea of joining the RCAF as the European conflict became a full fledged war. He rejected that idea when he learned that he might lose his U.S. citizenship as a result. He had no college degree and so was ineligible as a candidate for U.S. Army Aviation Cadets. But pilots were needed, and a change in requirements enabled him to master a two-year college equivalent test, and he subsequently applied for and was accepted as an Aviation Cadet.

Frank was an apt pupil, excelling in both flight and academic training, and ended up as Cadet Commander of his graduating class. He also ranked number four in Aerial Gunnery School. Although he had been told he could never become a fighter pilot because of his large athletic build, the need at the time of his graduation was such that he was assigned to P-51 training in Florida. His only mishap occurred when, on a photo-gunnery practice mission, his opponent threw a wrong switch and live ammunition resulted in Frank's being the only fighter pilot ever to be shot down over Florida.

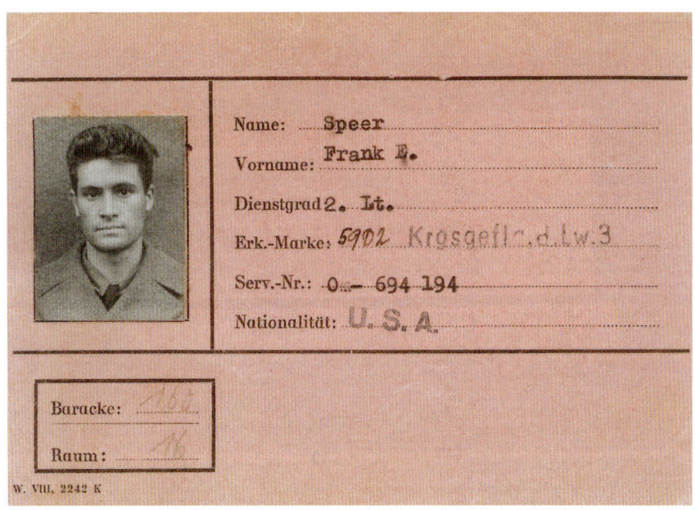

Name: Speer
Vorname: Frank E.
Dienstgrad 2. Lt.
Erk.-Marke: 5902 Krgsgefl[illegible].d.Lw.3
Serv.-Nr.: O – 694 194
Nationalität: U.S.A.
Baracke: [illegible]
Raum: [illegible]
W. VIII, 2242 K

After an arduous trip in an English banana boat across the winter-North Atlantic (the only bright spot of the day was afternoon tea and crumpets) he found himself in England. It was a country whose language replicated his own but it had to be relearned, as the English spoke it. It was also necessary to master one of the more difficult monetary systems in the world; thru-pence, shillings, pounds, farthings, etc.

He was assigned to the 4th Fighter Group, commanded by Colonel Don Blakeslee. He easily assimilated the aggressiveness and discipline of this outstanding Group and within a fairly short time became an Ace.

All went well until the return from a long escort mission to Poznan, Poland. It was Frank's 17th mission, and he was flying wingman to Kidd Hofer. Hofer's attitude had always been that rules were made to be broken, so as usual he left the Group and set off to find some action. Soon the two of them were strafing a *Luftwaffe* airdrome and, on the second pass, leaving three He-111s on fire, Frank's plane suffered a fatal hit by flak and he bellied in. He evaded capture and took off on foot for Denmark, hoping to stow away on a boat to Sweden. After eight days and nearly 400 miles across northern Germany as a scared fugitive, walking day and night with no food and no sleep, his body rebelled and he passed out. He was discovered by two German soldiers who immediately took him prisoner.

At Dulag Luft (interrogation center for downed enemy airmen) interrogation, threats, and solitary confinement proved unsuccessful for the Germans, and Frank was finally sent to Stalag Luft III for incarceration. He became a "Kriegie," the slang version of the German word *Kriegsgefangenen*, or prisoner of war. Conditions were barely tolerable, and it appeared they were systematically being starved to death. Fortunately the Red Cross provided supplemental food which the Germans sparingly parceled out to the Kriegies. Evidence of the effects of this program was borne out by the fact that Frank lost 67 pounds in his eleven months as a "guest" of the *Luftwaffe*.

In the bitter cold and snow of January, in the worst winter the Germans had seen in years, it appeared that a Russian offensive might liberate the camp. The Germans, however, wanted to retain the prisoners as bargaining chips in case of defeat. To that end, they marched the poorly-clad and poorly-shod Kriegies toward Nuremburg on what was to become a "death march," which scores did not survive. Even the guard dogs accompanying the marching column were gone after the first day, falling out with frozen feet.

The starving Kriegies who survived the brutal weather and lack of food and rest arrived at a small town after 77 hours of frozen hell, and were allowed to rest in an unheated factory. Then, after a seemingly endless train ride sandwiched into (standing room only) filthy 40 & 8 boxcars, they arrived at a camp outside of Nuremberg. It was over-crowded and unbelievably dirty, harboring almost every known species of fleas and lice.

Soon a drive by Patton's forces threatened to liberate the camp, and again the Kriegies were marched south toward Mooseburg. During this march Frank and a fellow Kriegie, Nelson Kennard, escaped twice, only to be recaptured. On their third try they were successful. They allied with some French forced laborers who hid them and stole food for them. The French helped in the capture of 24 German soldiers and an officer, and in holding them as prisoners until Patton's forces arrived and relieved them.

Patton's men, unconvinced that Frank and Nelson were not German spies, imprisoned them in a country schoolhouse, where they were to await word through "channels" as to their disposition. In the middle of the night an artillery duel convinced them this was not the kind of war they signed up for, and they broke out of their prison and hitchhiked back toward freedom. They were successful

in reaching Nuremberg, but from there the only travel available was by plane. The gravel agitator in charge of plane exits had to be bribed with their confiscated German souvenir pistols to convince him to assign them to a flight.

The flight ended at camp Lucky Strike in France, where they were deloused, their clothing burned, and they were admitted to the hospital. There was no means of escape across the Channel to England, but in due time they were loaded onto a hospital ship and embarked for the States. They left on the very day the Germans surrendered.

Back in the States Frank was sent on a State Department Mission, flying P-47s to Peru and training their pilots to fly them. Upon return Frank was scheduled to be sent to the Philippines, where he learned they were to live in tents. Frank decided, since he had never, even as a POW, lived in a tent in the service, it was time to cash in his points and say farewell to the military.

He returned to civilian life, went to college at night, and became an engineer with the Bell Telephone Co. Meanwhile, he bought a farm and he and his wife, Marjorie, raised and educated five children. The lack of promotions in the phone company and the absence of flight possibilities in his Reserve unit prompted Frank to resign both entities and to go into the food service business with two partners.

Their business was successful, and they eventually sold it to a national food service company. Frank became a regional manager with this company until he retired. Unable to be idle, Frank became a real estate agent but quit after a few years to focus on writing. This is his fourth book about the 4th Fighter Group and its exceptional people.

Frank now spends much of his time writing and speaking at schools, air shows, and meetings of various civic groups. He is active in veterans' organizations, serving as treasurer of the national P-51 Mustang Pilots Assoc. and Public Relations representative and Editor of "The Eagle Eye," the newsletter of the 4th Fighter Group Assoc. His health is such that he still plays doubles tennis two days a week and works out three.

He was credited with six enemy aircraft destroyed and earned the Distinguished Flying Cross, the Air Medal with three Oak Leaf Clusters, the Distinguished Unit badge, the POW medal, and the European Theatre Medal with one Star. He resides in Emmaus, Pennsylvania, with his wife Anne.

First Lieutenant **WILLIAM E. WHALEN**

William Whalen was born in 1922. From Hamilton, New York, he was commissioned and won his wings in the U.S. Army Air Forces in November 1943. He was assigned to the 355th Fighter Group July 1944, where he became known as "Gooney Bird." In the same month he was transferred to the 4th Fighter Group, 334 Squadron.

Colonel Claiborne H. Kinnard, Group Commander of the 355th., was transferred to the 4th Group, where he became commander in November 1944, while Colonel Blakeslee was on leave in the States. His job was to revitalize the 4th, which had lost most of its seasoned pilots by rotation, death, or by becoming POWs. He then exchanged some of the 4th's eager, but inexperienced, pilots for some of his combat savvy 355 Group pilots. William Whalen was one of the exchanged pilots.

In August, flying a P-51, he downed an Me-109 over France. The *Luftwaffe* was not very aggressive at that time, and having helped to get the 4th pilots on line, he applied for and returned to the 355th in August. He was credited with destroying three FW-190s on 26 November 1944 and became an Ace in February when he downed two Me-109s near Dessau.

No further records were found other than the fact that First Lt. Whalen eventually died in New York State.

He had eight victories and was decorated with the Silver Star, Distinguished Flying Cross, Purple Heart, and Air Medal with nine Oak Leaf Clusters.

Captain **VASSEURE H. WYNN**

Major John Godfrey dove alone on two bandits at one o'clock low. As he dropped his belly tank he discovered he had no wingman. He called on his radio "Come on down; cover me," as he closed on the rear Me-109. Unknown to Godfrey, the only one responding to his call was not from his 336 Squadron but was Captain Vasseure Wynn from 334 Squadron. Vasseure, nicknamed "Georgia," was not one to avoid a call for help, and he dove to Godfrey's rescue as Godfrey overshot his quarry. The German, at his lower speed was about to turn onto Godfrey's tail when Vasseure blazed away and downed him. Meanwhile Godfrey, flying his plane "Reggie's Reply," turned into the lead 109, blasting accurately and incessantly until the pilot bailed out. Wynn soon encountered another 109 and clobbered him prior to heading back to Debden.

Wynn was from Dalton, Georgia, and had transferred to the 4th Fighter Group from the RAF on 17 September 1943. He flew with the 334th Squadron until 13 April 1944, when he was shot down in his P-51B by an FW-190 and had to bail out, becoming a POW. His only satisfaction was in knowing that Captain "Nick" Megura immediately shot down his attacker.

Captain Wynn had five victories, 2 ½ with the RAF and 2 ½ with the 4th Fighter Group. He had the Distinguished Flying Cross and the Air Medal with one Oak Leaf Cluster. He had been Commanding Officer of "B" Flight for nearly a month prior to his becoming a POW. Later, as a Major, he became Commanding Officer of 466 Group in August 1953 at Misawa Air Base, Japan.

V

335th Fighter Squadron

The 335th Fighter Squadron was the offspring of No.121 Squadron of the British Royal Air Force. Formed 21 May 1941, No.121 was the second of the three Eagle Squadrons composed of American volunteers flying out of England. They were known as the "Chiefs" and were activated 12 September 1942, and assigned to the 4th Fighter Group based at Debden Airdrome, Essex, England.

They originally flew British Spitfires until they were replaced with P-47 Thunderbolts, which were in turn replaced by P-51 Mustangs a year later and were flown until war's end. The Chiefs were credited with destroying 262 enemy aircraft.

Shortly after VE Day the Chiefs were reassigned to Camp Kilmer, NJ, and were deactivated in November 1945. In September 1946 they were reactivated at Selfridge Field, Michigan. In April 1947 they moved to Andrews Air Force Base, MD, and were equipped with jet aircraft.

In November 1949 they deployed to Korea as the 4th Fighter Interceptor Wing, where they led their sister squadrons in destruction of enemy aircraft with 218.5 kills. In 1957, reassigned to Seymour Johnson, Air Base, NC, they participated in support of the Yom Kippur War. Later, they flew combat in the initial assault on Iraq, virtually halting the use of Iraq's Scud missiles. They remained in the theatre until June 1991. They continue to return to Southwest Asia to help enforce the U.N. sanctions against Iraq.

The "CHIEFS" Aces

1st Lieutenant **Charles F. Anderson**
Major **George Carpenter**
1st Lieutenant **George W. Ceglarski**
Major **William J. Daley**
Captain **Brack nmi Diamond**
Lt. Colonel **Roy W. Evans**
1st Lieutenant **Clemens A. Fiedler**
Major **James A. Happel**
1st Lieutenant **Loton D. Jennings Jr.**
Captain **Frank C. Jones**
Captain **Ted E. Lines**
Captain **Bernard J. McGrattan**
Major **Pierce W. McKennon**
F\O **Charles E. Poage Jr.**
1st Lieutenant **Paul S. Riley**
Captain **Albert L Schlegel**
Captain **Kenneth G. Smith**

1st Lieutenant **CHARLES F. ANDERSON**

Charles Anderson, from Indiana, flew with the famous 4th Fighter Group, 335th Squadron. He joined the squadron 11 August 1943. He flew P-47s and then P-51s in shooting down a mixed bag of *Luftwaffe* planes. He shot down Me-109s and Fw-190s, plus a Do-217 to make 10 aerial victories and destroyed five different kinds of planes on the ground for a total of 15.83 destroyed.

His P-47 was named "Hell's Belle," and his P-51 was called "Paul." His first victory was scored 30 January 1944 when, on an abortive bomber escort mission, the group was bounced by the *Luftwaffe*. Charles was the only one to score and he also damaged a second. On 29 March he destroyed 2 ½ Fw-190s to become an ace. On 12 April he became a double ace with the destruction of two Me-109s. Unfortunately Charles' luck ran out, as he was killed in action one week later.

He is credited with the Legion of Merit with one Oak Leaf Cluster, the Distinguished Flying Cross with four Oak Leaf Clusters, the Bronze Star, the Air Medal with 15 Oak Leaf Clusters, and the French *Croix de Guerre*.

Major **GEORGE CARPENTER**

Major Carpenter was born 14 May 1917 in Townsville, PA. He grew up in Oil City, where he graduated from high school in 1935. He attended Grove City College, meanwhile taking flight instruction under the Civilian Pilot Training Program.

George enlisted in the U.S. Army Air Corps in March 1941, assigned to class 42A. He unfortunately washed out when he fainted from the administration of a tetanus shot. He then contacted the Clayton-Knight Committee and subsequently joined the Royal Canadian Air Force. Upon completion of his training in California he was sent to England, where he flew Spits in No.121 (Eagle Squadron) in June 1942. He was in time to participate in the Dieppe raid in August.

In September 1942 he transferred to the U.S. 4th Fighter Group, 335 Squadron, where they began flying P-47s in early 1943. His first victory took place in February 1944, followed by four more in March to make him an Ace. By the end of April he added 8 1/3 more destroyed. Unfortunately, the last two of those were on the 18 April, when he paid the price of himself being shot down near Stendel, Germany. He became a POW in Stalag Luft III and later Mooseburg, near Munich. He was liberated in May 1945 and immediately returned to England, where he married his girlfriend before returning to the States.

He was 335 Squadron CO from February until his capture by the Germans and had destroyed 17.3 enemy aircraft. He had flown 143 sorties and 257 combat hours in Spitfires, P-47s, and P-51s. He had earned the Distinguished Flying Cross with Six Oak Leaf Clusters, the Air Medal with two Oak Leaf Clusters, the POW Medal, and the Presidential Unit Citation Medal.

When the war ended, he left the military service and attended Kirksville College of Osteopathy, graduating in 1956. He practiced medicine in Tennessee until his death in 2005.

Always a gentleman, he was proud of his time in the Air Force, and at a gathering of 4th Fighter Group retirees at Seymour Johnson Air Base shortly before his death, he was proud to show up wearing his wartime "Pinks and Greens," which still fit.

1st Lieutenant **GEORGE W. CEGLARSKI**

George was from Library, Pennsylvania, and arrived at the 4th Fighter Group 2 June 1944. He was there until 15 September. He was exchanged for pilots from the 355 Fighter Group that Lt. Colonel Kinnard brought in to help him reorganize and revitalize the 4th after Colonel Blakeslee was reassigned to the States.

Lieutenant Ceglarski had two victories with the 4th Group and three with the 355 Group.

Major **WILLIAM J. DALEY**

He enlisted from Amarillo, Texas, where he graduated from Amarillo High School and went to Amarillo College. He attempted to enlist in the Army Aviation Cadet program but was rejected. He then went to the Clayton Knight Committee, and having nearly 200 hours of flying time, was accepted for the RAF, where he graduated as a Pilot Officer 27 June 1941.

On 9 July he arrived in Glasgow, Scotland, and was off to an Operational Training Unit. Upon completion of his training 1 September he was assigned to No. 121 Squadron flying Hurricanes, soon transferring to Spitfires. He seldom encountered the *Luftwaffe* in their normal duties of convoy patrol and fighter sweeps. On 24 April, however, he shared in the destruction of a Junkers 52.

He soon downed an FW-190, and on 27 May he sank a minesweeper and destroyed another FW-190. In June he became acting flight lieutenant. On 29 September 1942, upon transfer to the USAAF, Major Daley became commander of 335 Squadron. In late 1942 he returned to the States and subsequently was assigned as Deputy Commander of the Ninth Air Force 371st Fighter Bomber Group.

In September 1944, while taxiing, he was rammed by an out of control P-47 and was killed. He had eight victories with the RAF and the 9th Air Force, but none with the 4th Group.

Captain **BRACK nmi DIAMOND**

Brack was assigned to the 4th Fighter Group, 335 Squadron 5 June 1944. He became "D" Flight Commanding Officer 16 September 1944. He had seven victories with the group and returned to the U.S. 13 January 1945. There is no further information available.

Roy Evans is pictured second from the right.

Lt. Colonel **ROY W. EVANS**

Roy Evans was the kind of pilot who avoided publicity but was always there when you needed him on a mission. He had overcome many obstacles in order to become a military pilot. As a youth, he was raised on a ranch near Santa Rosa, California, with a sister and two younger brothers. His parents separated, and it seemed inevitable that he and his siblings would be separated as well, but Roy refused to accept this outcome. Fortunately, an English couple offered to share their home with Roy and his siblings. Roy, being the eldest, worked very hard in order to keep his family together, and to show his gratitude to the couple who was so kind to them. He resolved to repay these people in some way as he grew older.

As a young man Roy obtained work with the Santa Fe Railroad as a special officer, and as a deputy sheriff. He later transferred to the engine service, where he remained until he saw the war clouds forming over Europe. While working at the railroad he wanted to be able to serve in defense of his country so he took Civilian Military Training, where he qualified as Sharp Shooter with the rifle and Expert with the machine gun. Roy had also managed to earn a pilot's license and attempted to join the Army Air Corps. He was turned down on the basis of his railroad job, which was considered vital to the country and exempted him from military service. Mindful of the dangerous position of the English as Hitler turned his wrath on them, Roy contacted the Clayton-Knight Committee, a group which was recruiting potential pilots for the Royal Air Force. He was accepted and went to Tulsa, Oklahoma, for training.

He earned the rank of Pilot Officer, graduating with the highest grades of anyone in the first six classes of recruits to graduate from that school, and was the only one in his class to graduate as a fighter pilot. He then went overseas to England for further training with the Royal Air Force in an Operational Training Unit. Again he excelled, and was the only one of his class to be assigned to #11 Group in the south of England, where the action was. Flying in defense of England, he felt very strongly that he was repaying the kind English couple who had taken his family into their home.

Roy found the English people to be very friendly and they treated him with respect. They did everything they could to make him feel at home, and were always willing to share what little they had. As an officer his word was his bond. He did not drink and was strictly a law-and-order guy; his only visible fault was a voracious appetite. The military equipment he received, although it was the best available was, unfortunately, well worn from the Battle of Britain. He flew a war-weary Spitfire which was constantly being written up as being not air worthy. Mindful of the general knowledge of its condition, his C.O., in a jovial mood, had suggested he should bail out of it. Roy's attitude was that since their pilots were outnumbered five-to-one, and put their lives on the line every day, he would do his job the best he could with whatever equipment they were able to supply. Roy loved to go on strafing trips, sometimes accompanied by Duane Beeson and sometimes with Frank Smolinski.

Later, as a Flying Officer, Roy sat down one Sunday to read the paper after having completed a combat mission over France and finishing a late supper. Suddenly the Tanoy announced that Pearl Harbor had been bombed. Since he was in the Eagle Squadron, he shortly found himself in the 4th Fighter Group with plenty of action, flying P-47s and later P-51s with their extended range. Roy enjoyed going on all the missions he could, even the tough ones.

On one occasion Roy was leading an escort mission to Paris where the Group destroyed 17 German planes, a record number for one day. Having finished their escort duties and being mindful of their low fuel situation they headed back toward England. They encountered a bomber group which was very late and unescorted and about to be attacked by a large formation of German fighters.

They turned into the Germans in a spread formation and from a long distance, though low on gas, they started firing their guns, knowing full well that the Germans were out of range. The audacious attack caused the Germans to turn and run for home. The bombers then turned and followed the fighters safely back to England. Roy received the Silver Star for this action.

As time went on Roy became an Ace, on the same mission, incidentally, as his friend Duane Beeson. He became C.O. of the 335th Squadron and attained the rank of Colonel. After his tour of 300 combat hours he applied for and was allowed an additional 25 hours before his mandatory return to the States. He was compelled to leave so hurriedly that he was unable to say farewell and thanks to all his English friends. He subsequently wrote a letter which he asked Jim Goodson to read to the next group of civilians he was to address. Upon completion of this duty Jim was given a standing ovation.

During his stay in England, in addition to his pilot and leadership duties, he had to contend with physical problems which caused hospitalization from time to time. Nevertheless he remained steadfast, doing his job as best he could at all times. He was proud of the fact that no British or German plane ever put a bullet hole in his plane, but occasionally American bombers took a crack at him. He did, however, have to bail out in the North Sea one time due to flak.

After Roy's last flight with the 4th Colonel Blakeslee told him General Anderson wanted to see him. General Anderson thanked him for his outstanding service and introduced him to eight others, all Generals or Colonels, who likewise thanked him. Officially, he ended that tour with eleven Distinguished Flying Crosses, two Purple Hearts, and innumerable Air Medals, in addition to his Silver Star and other awards, including the Distinguished Unit Award.

In the States he was assigned to where he was treated rather poorly, due possibly to jealously of his many combat ribbons and his two sets of wings. Eventually he underwent a serious operation there that alleviated, but did not cure, his physical problems.

Tiring of the Stateside duty he soon returned to England as Deputy C.O. of the 359th Fighter Group, becoming acting C.O. until some German ack-ack gunner found his target and Roy spent the balance of the European War as a POW. He had the dubious distinction of being the last of 37 Eagle Squadron pilots to become a POW. His stay caused him to go from a weight of 225 pounds to 167 pounds until he was liberated by General Patton's forces.

Roy is a dedicated gentleman, a steadfast warrior, a patriot, and an unsung hero. We should all be proud to have had him as a member of the 4th Fighter Group. I correspond with Roy, who lives in California and is in poor health.

1st Lieutenant **CLEMENS A. FIEDLER**

Clemens came to the 4th Group from Fredricksburg, Texas, 8 August 1943. He was assigned to the 335th Squadron. He had 50 missions completed when on 10 April 1944 his plane was hit by flak while strafing Romorantin Aerodrome, France.

His Mustang was streaming black oil and glycol and he attempted to bail out. His wingman watched as he climbed and put his kite on its back and then went into a dive. He leveled off for a few seconds and went into another dive with objects flying out of the cockpit. He was then seen hanging halfway out of the cockpit as his plane dove into the ground and he was killed.

Lt. Clemens was credited with 5.33 victories and had earned the Air Medal with one Oak Leaf Cluster.

Major **JAMES R. HAPPEL**

Major Happel was from Paulsboro, New Jersey, and joined the British Royal Air Force. He became a member of No.121 Eagle Squadron. He was assigned to the 4th Fighter Group, 335 Squadron 24 September 1942. He became Squadron Operations Officer 24 March 1944, and Commanding Officer 18 April of the same year. He finished his tour and returned to the States on 23 June 1944.

James left the USAAF in December 1945 and became a pilot for Allegheny Air. He retired to Berkeley Heights, NJ, where he died on 1 June 1970.

James had 8.7 victories and was awarded the Distinguished Flying Cross.

1st Lieutenant **LOTON D. JENNINGS JR**

Loton was from Wayne, Maine, and arrived at the 4th Group 20 October 1944. He was assigned to the 335th Squadron. Little was heard from him until April 1944, when he got one *Luftwaffe* plane on each of two missions, and then destroyed four on one Aerodrome shoot-up. In July he became "A" Flight Commanding Officer, and shortly thereafter he was transferred out of the group.

He had six planes to his credit and the Air Medal with four Oak Leaf Clusters.

Captain **FRANK C. JONES**

Frank Cazenova Jones, born in New York City, graduated from Army Air Corps pilot training 29 April 1942. He was assigned to the 4th Fighter Group, 335th Fighter Squadron, Debden, England, 25 March 1944. As a First Lieutenant with 650 flying hours he flew Mustangs.

His combat started in the spring of 1944 when he downed two *Luftwaffe* fighters in April and destroyed three on the ground. In May he downed two more and got 1 ½ on the ground and was appointed "D" Flight commander 8 May 1944, and "B" Flight commander on the 26th. Frank was promoted to Captain, and in June added two more 109s to his credit. August 8th was the end of Frank's career, as he destroyed a Ju-88 on an airfield in Norway and in turn was hit by flak and killed. His death came just ten days before he was to be married.

Captain Jones had 12 ½ enemy aircraft destroyed to his credit and was awarded the Distinguished Flying Cross with one Oak Leaf Cluster and the Air Medal with four Oak Leaf Clusters.

Captain **TED E. LINES**

Ted Elvan Lines was born in Mesa, Arizona, on 4 May 1921. He graduated from Aviation Cadet Training on 1 October 1943. He was assigned to the 4th Fighter Group, 335th Squadron in April 1944, and in May he shot down an Me-109 for his first victory. In August he shot down two more 109s while returning from an escort mission to Misburg, Germany. On 10 September he had a banner day as he became an Ace. Excerpts from his combat report show a remarkable picture:

"With engine trouble, I was alone, trying to catch up with our Group near Strasbourg. I saw seven 109s pass beneath me, a group of four followed by three, one of which was smoking. I called for help then dove on the one that was smoking, firing from 600 yards to 100 yards when the Hun went into the deck and exploded. I then turned to the one on the left which also exploded as he hit the deck. In the meantime, two got on my tail and I went into a tight orbit. At that time, six P-47s appeared and drove them off. I then turned on the third 109 which tried to do a short landing on an airdrome. He hit the ground with his wing flying off as I ran to avoid the flak. My R/T was out so I headed for home. I soon encountered a Ju-88 and as I fired on it three chutes appeared and the plane exploded."

On 17 September Ted was leading a section near Bucholt, Germany, when 15 Fw-190s bounced them from the rear and above:

"I broke, trying to discard my right external wing tank, and found myself head-on to five Fw-190s. I immediately started firing and one of them burst into flames. Still trying to drop my tank, two 190s flew under me going in the same direction as I. I got on the tail of one and started firing and the pilot bailed out. At this point a 190 closed on my tail, firing, hitting my tail and wing, and my wing tank finally came off. I went into orbit and after three orbits I was on the 190's tail. He broke for the deck with me close behind and I fired from 500 yards to 100 yards, hitting him all over his fuselage and wings. He burst into flames, exploding on impact with the ground."

Ted overcame two misfortunes, a faulty engine and a reluctant external wing tank, to achieve stunning victories over seven *Luftwaffe* planes in two missions.

Promoted to Captain, he continued to destroy *Luftwaffe* planes—three more in October—to end his combat victories. He had completed his combat tour in November and was assigned to the 70th Replacement Depot.

He subsequently left the Air Force and retired in his hometown of Mesa, Arizona.

Although Ted is officially credited with only ten victories, examination of combat reports indicates he actually destroyed 14. He had earned the Distinguished Service Cross, the Distinguished Flying Cross with one Oak Leaf Cluster, and the Air Medal with three Oak Leaf Clusters.

Captain **BERNARD J. McGRATTAN**

Bernard was from Utica, New York. Like many young men of the period he could not wait to fly in WWII. Prior to U.S. entry into the war he went north and joined the Royal Canadian Air Force. After earning his wings as a flying officer, he accumulated 286 hours prior to transferring to the U.S. Eighth Air Force on 26 May 1943.

He was assigned to the 4th Fighter Group, 335th Fighter Squadron with the commission of lieutenant in September. Flying P-47s, he scored his first victory in February 1944, shooting down an Fw-190. Shortly thereafter the group exchanged their P-47s for the new P-51 Mustangs. Bernard then shot down two twin engine planes in March and followed with 3 ½ victories in April. Meantime, he was appointed CO of "A" flight as he became an ace.

In May he blasted another Me-109, and becoming a Captain, he celebrated with the destruction of another Fw-190. Having completed his tour of combat with 9 victories to his credit, he had his bags packed for return to the States on leave. However, on 6 June, when he was scheduled to leave, he did not want to miss D-Day. He begged to be included in the invasion and was reluctantly assigned to lead Blue Flight on a mission near Rouen, France. They were flying on the deck strafing any targets of opportunity when suddenly, out of the low lying clouds, 10 plus enemy fighters appeared on their tails. With no room to maneuver, the four of them were shot down almost instantly and killed. The only one who escaped was Kidd Hofer, who had joined them as a fifth man in the flight.

Bernard had 8 ½ victories to his credit and had earned the Distinguished Flying Cross with two Oak Leaf Clusters, the Air Medal with four Oak Leaf clusters, and the Purple Heart.

Major **PIERCE W. "Mac" McKENNON**

Major McKennon, from Fort Smith, Arkansas, was born in Clarksville, Arkansas, 30 November 1919. He was educated in Fort Smith, where he excelled in music and sports. His father, a dentist, hoped he would follow a medical career; his mother wanted him to be a concert pianist, to which end he practiced seven hours a day, and she bribed him with a baby grand piano for his 16th birthday. As a senior in high school he won a music contest playing classics, earning him a four-year music scholarship to the University of Arkansas.

After a month in college he switched course and deserted the classics for the campus swing band. In his fourth year, in February 1941, he enlisted in the U.S. Army Air Corps as an Aviation Cadet. Sent to Hicks Field in Fort Worth, Texas, he trained in Stearman PT-17s, but washed out two months later with 29 flying hours due to extreme motion sickness. (I can relate to his difficulties; having endured primary training in a PT-19 in the gut-wrenching afternoon thermals generated by the hot Texas sun many cadets had the dubious pleasure of washing the residue of lunch from their planes upon landing.)

Not to be denied in his ambition to fly, a month later he enlisted in the RCAF. After some administrative type duties while awaiting a slot in the full flying training schedule, he finally was assigned to primary training, where he flew Fleet Finch biplanes. Passing all tests, he went on to gain his Pilot Wings in just four months rather than the usual ten to twelve months nomally expected.

In January 1942 he boarded a troop ship arriving in England on the 21st. In March he reported to an advanced pilot training unit, where he trained in Miles Masters and Hawker Hurricanes. He entered an Operational Training Unit in April to train in Supermarine Spitfires. In May, on a lark while flying a Spit, he pulled a low-level beat-up of his former training unit and returned to base, where he was immediately arrested and locked up. He spent two and a half days incarcerated pending a Court Martial. At the end of June he was found guilty of unauthorized aerobatics, reduced in rank, and stripped of his wings.

The authorities relented, for who knows what reason, and Mac was given a second chance, closely monitored for four months. On 14 October he won back his wings and was restored to his former rank of Sergeant Pilot. In November 1942, after one year and seven months in the RCAF/RAF, he was granted an honorable discharge to join the USAAF, and recommended as an above average pilot. He became a Second Lieutenant and spent three months learning to fly the P-47 Thunderbolt. He was assigned to the 4th Fighter Group, 335th Squadron in February 1943—at last, where he wanted to be, a fighter pilot. He christened his plane "Ridge Runner," his nose art being an Arkansas razorback hog.

As he participated in combat with the 4th the number of crosses painted on the nose grew, as did his reputation as a pianist. At any given moment in the Officers' Mess he would sit at the piano and pound out some of the most fantastic "Boogie Woogie" renditions, a cigarette hanging from his lip and a mug of beer staining the piano top. Often it would be his version of "A Slow Train Through Arkansas," with Deacon Hively sitting on the piano encouraging him.

Although he was an exceptionally good pilot, the Kraut flak gunners were not impressed, shooting him down twice and seriously wounding him on a third attempt. While strafing trains in August 1944 he was shot down. He evaded and was picked up by the French Maquis, who hid him and helped him to return to England a month later. Six months later, leading his Group, preparing to strafe Neubrandenberg Aerodrome flush with aircraft, again his plane was hit. He had no choice but to bail out about five miles from the aerodrome, landing in a small field near his crashed plane.

The Group watched and repelled German soldiers attempting to capture him. Lt. George Green, a crack flyer, who McKennon had been close to transferring out due to several rule infractions, proceeded to land to pick him up. It had never been done in a Mustang and it was strictly forbidden, a Court Martial awaiting anyone attempting to do it, but that did not deter Green. He landed and immediately disposed of his parachute and dinghy, allowing the six-foot-one McKennon to sit in the cockpit with Green on his lap, flying the plane. The bumpy field was short and Green called upon every last ounce of power capable of the Rolls/Royce engine at 60 inches of mercury manifold pressure to gather the minimum take-off speed necessary to get them over the trees at the end of the run. With about one-third of a normal run they barely cleared the trees and headed for England to the cheers of the watching Group. McKennon calmly assured the Group that "Horseback is airborne again, okay fellows, form up and let's go home!"

On the way back to Debden they encountered a dense haze that required them to climb higher and higher, since Green, with his face above and forward of the instrument panel, could not see the instruments to fly through the haze. They got above the haze at 18,000 feet and had to share their one oxygen mask to remain conscious. Arriving back at Debden, the tower operator was astounded to hear their request for landing instructions for two!

Again strafing Rosenheim-Gahlingen Aerodrome on 16 April 1945, McKennon was hit by an explosive round in the cockpit, wounding his head and neck and causing profuse bleeding. He managed to land at a forward base, where they bandaged his wounds and advised him to not fly back to Debden. He ignored the advice, leading his Squadron home and completing, for him, his last combat mission, as the Germans surrendered before his wounds healed enough for him to fly again.

After 560 combat hours, being shot down and evading twice, scoring 21 plus victories, and being Squadron CO for eight months; having been washed-out of U.S. flight training, losing his RCAF wings by Court Martial, and regaining them, his luck ran out. In June 1947 he was killed in a tragic flying accident.

Pierce had 21.68 enemy aircraft to his credit and had received the Distinguished Flying Cross with four Oak Leaf Clusters, the Air Medal with 16 Oak Leaf Clusters, the Purple Heart, and the French *Croix de Guerre*. He was truly an unusual man. He remained in the USAF, but was killed in a flying accident on 18 June 1947.

F/O **CHARLES E. POAGE, JR.**

Charles Poage arrived at the 4th Fighter Group on 13 July 1944. He was assigned to the 335th Squadron. During September, he accounted for four Huns destroyed and then in December the Group, returning from a mission on 24 December, was prevented from landing at Debden due to inclement weather. They ended up at Raydon, where they spent the night.

On Christmas Day, still unable to return to Debden, the group flew a mission from Raydon to support bombers in the Bonn/Trier area. Thirty-plus *Luftwaffe* fighters were encountered and the 4th shot down twelve of them. Unfortunately, two of our fighters were shot down; Charles Poage had to bail out and became a POW. Donald Emerson, who had shot down two of the enemy aircraft, was shot down and killed by anti-aircraft fire.

Charles Poage had six victories to his credit.

1st Lieutenant. **PAUL S. RILEY**

Paul S. (Rip) Riley was born 17 February 1919 in York, PA. He attended Pennsylvania State University in 1937-38. With the outbreak of WWII in Europe he went to Canada to join the Royal Canadian Air Force in October 1941 and received his wings in August 1942. He remained with the RCAF and was attached to a Royal Air Force Squadron flying Spitfires and Hurricanes while stationed in Scotland.

In May 1943 he transferred to the U.S. Army Air Corps. In September he was assigned to the 4th Fighter Group, 335th Fighter Squadron. He checked out in the P-47 Thunderbolt and claimed his first victory, an Me-110 downed near Koblenz, on 20 February 1944. The Group transferred into P-51Bs and he was credited with downing an Me-109 on 4 March and damaging one the next day. On 16 March he shot down one Me-110 and damaged another southwest of Munich. He completed the month with the destruction of an Me-109 north of Ulzen on the 29th.

On 5 April the Fourth swept deep into Germany and attacked *Luftwaffe* airfields in the Berlin area and destroyed 43 aircraft on the ground and two in the air, one being an He-111 downed by Riley. Three days later, escorting bombers to industrial targets in Brunswick, the Group was bounced by 100 plus German fighters near Celle. In the ensuing battle the Fourth claimed 31 enemy aircraft destroyed, including an Fw-190 credited to Riley. On the 10th he added a Bu-131 trainer to his score and shared a 109 on the 22nd.

Two days later, near Worms, Germany, the squadron was jumped by 35-plus Fw-190s. The squadron destroyed 10 of them. Riley downed one Fw-190 and collided with another, shearing off one-quarter of his left wing. The Jerry bailed out, but Riley was able to recover and control his plane, and he started for home at 4,000 feet. He was then hit by flak and bailed out, landing about 60 yards from the ack-ack battery that shot him down. It was fortunate because he was injured and they picked him up, immediately taking him to a hospital. He languished in captivity for several days before they properly cared for his broken leg. He then became a POW, incarcerated in Stalag Luft III after the usual interrogation at Dulag Luft. At Stalag Luft III, with his broken leg recovering, he suffered the usual lack of proper nutrition, eventually losing 45 pounds.

Riley was fortunate in not being on the winter march out of Sagan to avoid release by the advancing Russians. He, with other disabled prisoners, was transported by overcrowded 40 & 8 boxcars to a destination at a Stalag near Nuremberg. Later in the spring the camp was evacuated, and the Kriegies were marched to Mooseburg. On this march he engaged in a couple of abortive escapes which were not successful, and he wound up in the Stalag at Mooseburg. Shortly thereafter the camp was liberated by Patton's warriors. He was then transported to Camp Lucky Strike, France, where he was treated, deloused, clothed, and sent to the States by ship, arriving the day after VE Day.

He was credited with 9.5 enemy aircraft destroyed. He was awarded the Purple Heart, the Distinguished Flying Cross with 4 Oak Leaf Clusters, and the Air Medal with 3 Oak Leaf Clusers. Following his release from service in 1945, he later worked for the Ballistics Research Laboratory at the Aberdeen Proving Grounds, Maryland.

Captain **ALBERT L. SCHLEGEL**

Albert Schlegel was born in Cleveland, Ohio, in 1919. He joined the British Royal Air Force, transferring to the U.S. Army Air Corps in January 1943. He had the rank of Flight Officer. He was stationed at Debden and flew Spitfires until they were replaced by P-47s in March 1943. He was assigned to the 335th Fighter Squadron and was promoted to 1st Lieutenant.

His first victory occurred on 2 October 1943, an Me-109. In March 1944 the group switched to P-51s and Schlegel became a Flight Leader. His activities picked up, and he began to have victories to the extent that he became an ace on 22 April, and two days later he added two 109s and shared a third. Now a Captain, he went on leave to the U.S. When he returned he became 335's Squadron Operations Officer, an office he held for only ten days, ending with him being shot down by flak and killed on 28 August.

He had scored 13 ½ confirmed and 2 ½ probables. He had earned the Distinguished Flying Cross with four Oak Leaf Clusters and the Air Medal with three Oak Leaf Clusters.

Captain **KENNETH G. SMITH**

Captain Smith was from Boise, Idaho, and was born 8 June 1914. He attended the College of Idaho, then worked for the Idaho Power Co. About 1940 he moved to California. He joined the Army Aviation Cadet program, but left abruptly and was accepted by the Clayton Knight Committee. He received his flight training and was commissioned 19 January 1942. Assigned to No.121 Eagle Squadron, he arrived at the 4th Group, 335 Squadron as they were organizing in October 1942.

He had accumulated five enemy aircraft victories when, on a Rhubarb to the Bordeaux area of France 21 March 1944, he was shot down by flak and became a POW. Subsequently it was learned that he had been badly burned about his face and a German surgeon did an excellent plastic surgery reconstruction of everything but his eyebrows. He was adamant in refusing an operation on his eyebrows; he said "No German eyebrows, I'll wait and get American eyebrows." While recuperating he was an orderly in Dulag Luft and received proper treatment.

Upon return he stayed in the Air Force and became CO of 37th Fighter Group, at Dow Field, Bangor, Maine. On 20 October 1947 he was killed in a crash of a disabled P-47 on 20 October 1970 when he remained at the controls to avoid crashing into a populated area.

VI

336th Fighter Squadron

The 336 Fighter Squadron was constituted by the War department 22 August 1942, and was activated at Bushey Hall, England, on 12 September. It had been designated as No. 133 Eagle Squadron, and was made up of American volunteers to the British Royal Air Force. They were transferred to the U.S. Fourth Fighter Group, based at Debden Aerodrome, Essex, England, and they were known as the Rocketeers.

The Squadron flew British Spitfires until American P-47 Thunderbolts became available in sufficient numbers to equip the group in 1943. A year later the group was re-equipped with P-51 Mustangs, which became the standard until the end of the war.

The 336th Squadron was credited with the destruction of 358 enemy aircraft. The group was deactivated at Camp Kilmer, New Jersey, 10 November 1945 after war's end.

The unit was reactivated in September 1946 and has remained on duty under various Commands to this day. They were equipped with F-80s and eventually F-86s. During a tour in Korea they destroyed 116.5 enemy aircraft prior to returning to the States and being assigned to Seymour Johnson AFB, North Carolina. There they flew F-100s and then F-105s. In 1967 they manned F-4D Phantom IIs in support of operations during the Pueblo incident.

In 1972 and 1973 the Rocketeers deployed to Ubon Royal Thai Air Base, Thailand, in support of the Southeast Asia conflict. One month after returning to the States, in October 1973 they were called upon to support Israel during the Yom Kippur War. In 1989 the Rocketeers became the first operational F-15E Strike Eagle squadron in the Air Force.

In 1990 the squadron deployed to Southeast Asia in response to the Iraqi invasion of Kuwait. During the next four years they had four 90 day rotations to the area, and by the end of Desert Storm they had dropped 6.5 million pounds of ordinance on enemy targets.

The "Rocketeers" Aces

Captain **Carl R. Alfred**
Flight Officer **Donald P. Baugh**
Major **Joseph H. Bennett**
Captain **Kendall E.Carlson**
Colonel **Van E. Chandler**
Captain **Melvin N. Dickey**
Captain **Donald R. Emerson**
Colonel **Vermont Garrison**
Major **Fred W. Glover**
Major **Don Salvadore Gentile**
Major **John Trevor Godfrey**
Major **James A. Goodson**
Colonel **Leroy Gover**
Captain **Harry N. Hagan**
Captain **Robert D. Hobert**
Colonel **Joseph H. Joiner**
1st Lieutenant **Gilbert L. Kesler**
Captain **Willard W. Millikan**
Major General **Carroll W. McColpin**
Lt. Colonel **Robert F. Nelson**
Lt. Colonel **William J. O'Donnell**
1st Lieutenant **Douglas P. Pederson**

Captain **CARL R ALFRED**

Carl was from Atwater, Ohio, and was assigned to the 4th Fighter Group, 336 Squadron from July 1944 to 16 April 1945.

While strafing Praha Aerodrome in Czechoslovakia his plane was hit by flak, went into a shallow dive, and exploded upon crashing. Alfred was killed in the crash. He had eight victories to his credit and was awarded the Distinguished Flying Cross.

Flight Officer **DONALD P. BAUGH**

Donald enlisted from Sioux City, Iowa, and was assigned to the 4th Fighter Group, 336 Squadron. He served from 17 November 1944 to 21 July 1945, at which time he was transferred. He retired from the Air Force as a Major.

He was credited with five enemy aircraft destroyed.

Major **JOSEPH H. BENNETT**

Bennett was from Morton, Texas, and was born 25 November 1918. He attended Abilene Christian College, Abilene, Texas, and Eastern New Mexico University prior to enlisting in the Army Air Corps on 25 April 1941. He was commissioned a Second Lieutenant and received his wings in class 41-I at Stockton Field, California, 31 December 1941.

He was assigned to the 54th Fighter Group flying P-39s. In March 1943 he was transferred to the 356th Fighter Group, 360th Fighter Squadron at Groton Field, Connecticut, flying P-47s. His next stop was Goxhill, England, in August.

As a Captain he was assigned to the 56th Fighter Group, the most formidable rival of the Fourth, where he had his first victory, an Me-110 on 20 December. On 8 March 1944, in an encounter with 100-150 *Luftwaffe* fighters, he downed two Me-109s and an Fw-190 to become an Ace.

In April he transferred to the 4th Fighter Group, where he flew a P-51 "Lucky Ann."

On the 15th he had a collision in the clouds and bailed out into the North Sea with a broken shoulder. He was soon picked up by a Walrus (an amphibious rescue plane) and returned to base.

On 25 May he destroyed two Me-109s and two Fw-190s. He was then rammed by a frustrated *Luftwaffe* pilot in a 109 which severed his tail section, and he bailed out to become a POW for the rest of the war.

Joe was promoted to Major prior to leaving active duty in January 1946. He took up farming in west Texas. After 10 years he moved to Clifton, Texas, and operated a resort on Lake Whitney. After 20 years with the U.S. Army Corps of Engineers he retired in 1980.

Bennett had 8 1/2 planes to his credit and earned the Distinguished Flying Cross with two Oak Leaf Clusters, the Purple Heart, and the Air Medal with three Oak Leaf Clusters.

Captain **KENDALL E. CARLSON**

"Swede," as he was known, came from Red Bluff, California, and was born 14 July 1919. He joined the Royal Canadian Air Force and earned his wings in December 1940. When the U.S. established the 4th Fighter Group in England Swede joined them in March 1943. He was assigned to 336 Squadron flying P-47s, with which he scored his first victory. Later, flying the new Mustangs, Swede knocked down three Me-110s in furious battles during March 1944.

On 22 April his flight attacked 20-plus Me-109s. He chased one down to the deck and destroyed it to become an Ace. On 25 February 1945, while strafing Kothen Airdrome, he crash landed on the airfield but climbed out on the wing to direct the rest of the destruction. He was taken prisoner and headed for POW incarceration, where he remained until war's end.

After he was released and returned to the States, he next became involved in the Korean War, where he flew combat missions with the 12th Fighter-Bomber Squadron from July 1950 to January 1951. During this time he was promoted to Lt. Colonel. He left the Air Force in April 1951 and returned to Red Bluff, where he lived until his death in 1977.

Carlson had credit for ten *Luftwaffe* planes destroyed and earned the Distinguished Flying Cross with Oak Leaf Cluster and the Air Medal.

Colonel **VAN E. CHANDLER**

He was born 5 March 1925 in Waxahachie, Texas. He became an Aviation Cadet in February 1943 and graduated as a pilot at Aloe Field, Texas, in January 1944. He transitioned to P-51s in Florida and then shipped to England. On 6 June 1944 (D-Day), he was assigned to the 4th Fighter Group, 336 Squadron, and entered combat during the invasion of France.

Van had two victories by Christmas and added two more on Christmas Day. His fifth victory came on New Year's Day 1945, making him an Ace at the tender age of 19. Flying a Mustang named "Wheezy," he bailed out over Allied lines in Europe, but was uninjured.

After WWII, he remained in the Air Force and was sent to Korea in 1951, where he flew F-86s in the 51st Fighter Group, 25th Fighter Squadron. There he scored three victories over MiG-15s in early 1952. Later, while engaged in the Vietnamese Conflict, he was promoted to Colonel and then, flying F-100s, he was named Deputy Commander for Operations of the 31st Tactical Fighter Wing.

Chandler retired in 1974, having scored nine kills in WWII, followed by three in Korea. He earned the Legion of Merit, the Distinguished Flying Cross, and the Air Medal with 12 Oak Leaf Clusters.

Captain **MELVIN N. DICKEY**

Enlisted from Tampa, Florida, Melvin was assigned to 336 Squadron from 12 July 1944 to 6 June 1945, at which time he was transferred to the U.S.

His plane was named "Betty Jane II," and he was credited with the destruction of five enemy aircraft.

Captain **DONALD R. EMERSON**

Born 17 May 1923, Donald was raised on a farm in Minnesota during the Great Depression. He graduated from high school in 1941, not having excelled to any spectacular degree academically. He definitely did not feel destined to be a farmer, so he soon moved to Chicago to find work. Jobs were scarce, but a friend got him a position at Montgomery Ward and took him in as a boarder. At Christmas, although not previously interested in flying, he took his first airplane ride.

With the advent of the Pearl Harbor attack he felt that he or his brother would be drafted. Donald, not interested in running the farm, decided to enlist so his older brother would be deferred to attend to that duty.

He chose the Army and was sworn in July 1942. He was assigned to the Air Corps and shipped to Lowery Field, Colorado, to become an armorer. Although his academic background was weak, he applied for and was accepted as an Aviation Cadet. In October 1942 he was sent to Nashville, Tennessee, for Primary Training, and after Basic and Advanced Training he graduated as a Second Lieutenant 1 October 1943.

After further training in fighters in Florida he shipped to New York City to embark on the *Isle de France* bound for England. There he became attached to the prestigious 4th Fighter Group. He flew Mustangs and had his embellished with a fighting-mad "Donald Duck" image.

Donald was big-hearted and wore a perpetual smile. He was soon endeared by his comrades as a friend and a leader. During 89 combat missions escorting bombers, strafing, etc., he destroyed seven enemy aircraft and wrought destruction on many trains, trucks, and other surface targets, becoming an Ace and a Captain in the process. He flew combat on D-Day and participated in the Russian Shuttle mission. When his first tour ended he volunteered for a second.

On 24 December 1944 the Group flew an uneventful escort mission to Giessen. Upon returning to England they discovered Debden was socked in tight with impenetrable fog, so the Group landed at Raydon. The pilots were extremely disappointed at not being able to return to their base for the annual Christmas celebration, where 250 British Blitz orphans were treated to a grand party with entertainment, gifts, food, ice cream, cake, and a visit from Santa Claus.

Debden base rallied to the occasion and sent a truck loaded with four turkeys, cigarettes, whiskey, money, and blankets to the pilots at Rayden to help restore their Christmas spirit.

Unfortunately, the business of the following day called for an escort mission, this one to the Bonn/Trier area. Thirty-plus 109s and 190s tried to attack the bombers out of the sun but were immediately engaged by the 4th Group escort. Twelve enemy aircraft were destroyed, but one of the Group's pilots joined the ranks of the MIA list.

Donald became detached from the group and was seen to engage six Me-109s single-handed, downing two of them; and then, out of ammunition, he headed for home on the deck. He failed to return to base and was later found dead in the wreckage of his plane in Belgium, the victim of ground fire. Donald had the unenviable distinction of being the only 4th pilot to be killed on Christmas day. He was buried in his flying clothes the following day at the age of 21.

Donald was awarded the Distinguished Flying Cross with two Oak-leaf Clusters, the Air medal with one silver and two bronze Oak-leaf Clusters, and the Purple Heart.

Colonel **VERMONT GARRISON**

Vermont was born in Mount Victory, Kentucky, on 29 October 1915. He attended Eastern Kentucky State University and then went to England and volunteered with the Royal Air Force. Assigned to the Eagle Squadrons, which were made up primarily of U.S. volunteers, he flew Spitfires and Hurricanes before transferring in July 1943 to the newly formed U.S. Army Air Force 4th Fighter Group. There he was assigned to the 336 Squadron, where he flew P-47s and P-51s.

His first victory was on 16 December 1943, and by February he had achieved four more victories and had become an Ace. A month later he was shot down by ground fire and spent the rest of the war as a POW.

After the war ended Garrison remained in the service as a Captain. He trained and flew in jet aircraft and led the winning team of P-80s in the world-wide gunnery meet in 1948 at Nellis Air Force Base, Nevada. Later, he led the 4th Fighter Group's jet demonstration team of F-80s and later F-86s.

During the Korean War he commanded the 3596 Training Squadron at Nellis for two years. Back in combat in Korea, he was 4th Group Commander of 335 Fighter Squadron. He shot down his first MiG in February 1953 and became a Korean War Ace in June. He then became a double Ace one month later with his 10th victory only eight days before the war ended.

Promoted to Colonel in 1961, he returned to combat for the third time in 1966 as Vice Commander of the 8th Tactical Fighter Wing. There he flew F-4C Phantoms out of a base in Ubon, Thailand. He retired in 1973, one of only seven to achieve Ace status in two wars.

In February 1994 he suffered a fatal heart attack at Mt. Home, Idaho.

He had 7 ½ victories in WWII and 10 in Korea. He earned the Distinguished Service Cross, the Silver Star with an Oak Leaf Cluster, the Legion of Merit with an Oak Leaf Cluster, the Distinguished Flying Cross with six Oak Leaf Clusters, the Bronze Star with two Oak Leaf Clusters, the Purple Heart, and the Air Medal with many Oak Leaf Clusters.

Major **FRED W. GLOVER**

Fred Glover hailed from Ashville, North Carolina. He had played a little professional baseball but never had much to say about it.

He had once seen a Flying Tigers pilot return home, and he was so impressed with the adulation he received that Fred never forgot it. He decided that flying was the service for him. Fred and several of his buddies decided to enlist and headed for Fort McPherson, Georgia. They tried to enlist in the Army Air Corps for cadet training but were told the Army had no use for them. Glover replied, "Well, to hell with you friend" and stalked out.

His passion carried him to the Royal Canadian Air Force, where he earned his wings. He was assigned to England to ferry planes, not to combat. He was totally dissatisfied with this; he wanted to be a fighter pilot. When they ignored his request Fred took an Oxford transport up and power-dived it. It was not exactly what this type of aircraft was designed to do, and the damage to the plane and the arrogance of the pilot did not sit well with the authorities; so, on 20 February 1944 he was sent to the 4th Group to fly combat.

Upon arriving at his new assignment Fred immediately had a little altercation with Col. Don Blakeslee, the Commanding Officer, at the bar when Blakeslee made a slightly derogatory remark about Glover being a "Lightning" ferry pilot. Glover was not one to silently accept derision and replied that he felt he could fly a plane as well as anyone else present, "SIR." The conflict was resolved with Blakeslee having another drink and Glover abstaining. However, they were soon to become good friends when Blakeslee discovered that Glover liked fighting the Germans as much as he did.

On 30 April, while strafing Lyon/Bron Airdrome, Glover's plane was hit by flak, causing him to lose his glycol (coolant). He had to bail out, but he evaded capture, meeting up with some French resistance Fighters who sheltered him until he finally returned to England on 28 May.

In August '44 he became Squadron Commander of 336, where he had an intense rivalry with "Red Dog" Norley, his roommate and Commander of 335 Squadron, both eager to be the top scoring Squadron in the Group. Glover never gave up; he was a great pilot and intensely aggressive, which was much admired by his squadron pilots and kept their morale at a constant high.

In June 1945 he was transferred to 8th Air Force Headquarters, ending his combat.

He had 22.8 enemy aircraft to his credit and had earned the Silver Star, the Distinguished Flying Cross with Oak Leaf Clusters, and the Air Medal with Oak Leaf Clusters. He was killed in a flying accident in July 1956 in Hazlehurst, Georgia.

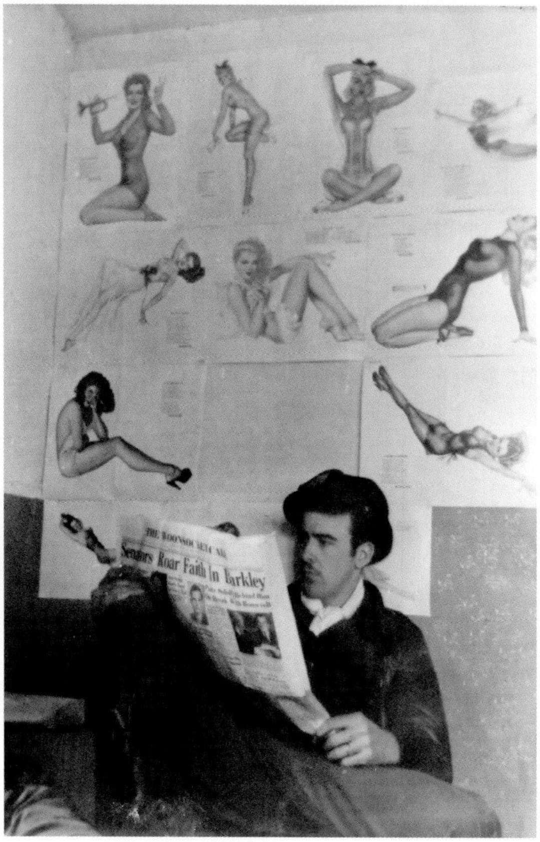

Major **DON SALVADORE GENTILE** and Major **JOHN TREVOR GODFREY**

Fate, success, and publicity combined to inexorably bind together these two officers in 4th Fighter Group history, as well as in the minds of the wartime American civilians whose adulation of them was nationwide.

Fate cast a common bond between the two men who shared much in their military background: both lacked the educational requirements necessary to join the U.S. Army Air Corps; both then joined the Royal Canadian Air Force and were later assigned to the British Royal Air Force; both became Eagle Squadron members, and then were welcomed into the 4th Fighter Group when it was activated in 1942. They met when they were both assigned to the 336th Fighter Squadron.

Don Gentile, of Piqua, Ohio, was born 6 December 1920. While in high school he played football and nourished an addiction for speed. He was well known by the police, who could never catch him as he sped along in his father's Lincoln-Zephyr. He also yearned to fly, and saved money while working as a waiter in his father's restaurant in order to buy a plane and take flying lessons. He purchased a nine-cylinder craft, much to his father's chagrin, and his father returned it when tests found that it was not even airworthy. To solve the problem his father bought an Aero-Sport biplane for Don. He immediately started to buzz everything in sight until the police threatened to jail him if he did not stop.

Unable to qualify for the United States Army Air Corps, he enlisted in the Royal Canadian Air Force in July 1941. He traveled to England aboard the *S.S. Letitia* and arrived five days after Pearl Harbor. He trained in British Miles Masters, Hurricanes, and Spitfires; graduated in November 1941 as a Pilot Officer; and showed such flying ability that he was assigned as an instructor to make the best use of his skills. This definitely was not his cup of tea; he wanted to fly in combat. Frustrated, he beat up a greyhound racetrack at near ground level while races were in progress. Pandemonium followed as spectators and dogs departed in mass confusion. He was confined to quarters, and his commanding officer amended his file to the effect that he was not fit to be an instructor by reason of temperament.

He was transferred to No. 133 Squadron, commanded by Col. Donald Blakeslee. This was one of the three squadrons of American volunteers known as the Eagle Squadrons. His first combat mission was on 22 June 1942 flying a Spitfire, but missions were uneventful, with Don sticking close to his element leader. However, on 31 July things changed. His squadron was escorting RAF "Bostons" attacking Abbeville Airfield, home of the famous German JG-26. Don's flight was attacked by Fw-190s and his leader was shot down, blowing up and leaving Don alone. He was immediately attacked, and in desperation hauled back on the stick, going into a spiral dive and evading his attackers. He then flew back alone to land at Gravesend. His luck changed in August when he destroyed a Ju-88 and an Fw-190 that were attacking ships evacuating survivors from the Dieppe landing. Shortly thereafter, with the United States' entry into the war, Don accepted the USAAF offer of a commission, joined the 4th Group, and was

assigned to the 336 Squadron. He christened his assigned plane "Shangri-La."

John Trevor Godfrey was born in Montreal, Canada, and raised in Woonsocket, Rhode Island. Rejected by the USAAF for lack of college requirements, at 18 he ran away to Canada to join the Montreal Regiment, but was returned by his father, who eventually consented to his joining the Royal Canadian Air Force.

John was handsome; impressive at 6' 2", with dark hair and piercing black eyes with the unusual ability to pick out and identify planes at great distances. He trained in the RCAF in Canada, graduating in October 1942 as a Sergeant Pilot. Ordered to the Royal Air Force in England, he arrived 9 November 1942. Following training in Miles Masters and Spitfires, he was promoted to Pilot Officer in March 1943. He then transferred to the USAAF in September 1943 as a 2nd Lt. and was assigned to the 4th Fighter Group, 336 Squadron, flying P-47s. He christened his plane "Reggie's Reply" in honor of his brother Reginald, who was killed in October 1941 when his ship, bound for England, was torpedoed by a German U-Boat.

John was soon "adopted" by a dog named "Lucky" who became his constant companion. Lucky enjoyed flying and accompanied John on many of his "peaceful" sorties. On one occasion when John landed at a distant airfield, he left Lucky in the cockpit while he went about his business. The ground crew saw the plane with 20 crosses on the fuselage and a dog in the cockpit and concluded the pilot had brought his "Seeing eye Dog" with him.

Godfrey stuck close to his leader on many uneventful flights until the first of December 1943, when he got his first kill, a 109. On 22 February 1944 the group received its first Mustang, greatly improving the morale of the pilots, many of whom were not happy with the P-47, a seven-ton behemoth they'd been flying.

On the eighth of March, on an escort mission to Berlin, with some of the P-51's bugs still not completely resolved, Godfrey was leading a section of four with Gentile leading another. Aborts decimated the sections, as one by one they were forced to drop out and head for home. Finding themselves alone the two joined forces, with Godfrey flying Gentile's wing. When they arrived over Berlin the heavies were being pounded by intense flak and scores of enemy fighters. The sky was full of parachutes as the bombers were crippled by sustained fighter attacks. The two joined the fray and one after another they shot down enemy aircraft, covering each other as one or the other latched on to a German fighter. Godfrey ran out of ammunition and Gentile was almost out when they shot down their sixth plane. Gentile had scored 3 ½ and Godfrey 2 ½ destroyed. They headed back to England, but soon encountered a

lone crippled B-17 limping its way home from combat, a "sitting duck" for any enemy fighter. Although they were now impotent without ammunition, they formed up aside the Fort as a deterrent and shepherded it to the safety of the cloud cover over the Channel. They then gunned it back to Debden.

Their teamwork had been so successful they decided to team up as much as possible; and, to help recognize one another in combat, they had a red-and-white checkerboard design painted on each side of the cowling beneath the exhaust ports on both 51s. This made "Shangri-La" and "Reggie's Reply" easily identified in the melee of battle.

On 5 April 1944 Gentile added five more victories to his credit. The man who never took leave when he was eligible now had a score of 27.8 official victories, almost two more than Eddie Rickenbacker's record of 26 in WWI. On the 11th, General Eisenhower visited the base and awarded Gentile and Colonel Blakeslee the Distinguished Service Cross, calling Gentile a "One Man Airforce." Word of his accomplishment soon spread, and on the 13th the media converged on the base to shoot pictures of this new hero as he returned from an escort mission to Schweinfurt. The man who loved to buzz decided to put on a show for the cameramen. As the cameras recorded his every move he dropped lower and lower, heading for them at high speed. Unfortunately he did not compensate for the slight rise in the middle of the field and his prop and radiator scoop clipped the ground. The plane bounced up and smashed down several hundred feet away, a piece of junk with a broken back. Miraculously, the pilot's only injury was to his pride. It is rumored that all film was confiscated and only occasional stills shot by nearby spectators seem to have survived.

Don, the pilot who had flown 184 combat sorties and been awarded 26 decorations, including the Distinguished Service Cross, British and American Distinguished Flying Crosses, the Italian equivalent of the Silver Star, and was later to be inducted into the Aviation Hall of Fame was, however, not immune to Col. Blakeslee's dictum, "Anyone pranging a plane while buzzing will not fly with us again"; he was destined to be grounded until orders were cut sending him to the States on a War Bond tour. Since the Air Force was stressing teamwork, it was decided to have Godfrey, whose score now stood at 26 and who had been promoted to Captain, accompany him as the other half of this very successful team. After an impressive tour showing America how their homeland sacrifices helped the "Troops" do their dangerous jobs, visits to their families, and general relaxation, it was time to return to work. Gentile, his combat career finished, was assigned to Wright-Patterson Airfield as a test pilot. Godfrey was assigned to Training Command, where he was looked upon as being "over the hill" by his youthful students. To show how combat flying really looked, he vented his frustration with a low combat pass, completely obliterating the ground target. He soon received orders returning him to combat with the 4th.

On 5 August 1944, back to what he did best, he blew up eight locomotives, damaged planes on the ground, and demolished a 109 with only two of his guns firing, the other two out of ammo. His plane had been damaged from debris and ground fire while strafing the airfield, a fact he chose to ignore. The next day his plane again was heavily damaged, and he wore his hand raw using his priming pump to force raw gas to the engine in order to keep it from overheating to the point of seizure as he nursed his plane back to Debden.

On 24 August he spotted a row of Ju-52s on an airfield and flamed four of them. As he turned, he accidentally flew across the line of fire of the six-fifties his wingman was firing at another target, completely demolishing his engine. He bellied in and headed away on foot, but to no avail. He was soon captured and wound up in Stalag Luft III, site of the mass breakout in what was known as the "Great Escape."

Returning to the States upon liberation, he met Gentile and eventually the two of them, tired of non-combat Army life, resigned their commissions in January 1946 to take jobs marketing civilian aircraft.

They soon also tired of this and both quit. Don went back to the Army Air Force, but in January 1951, out of Andrews AFB, Maryland, he was flying a T-33 which lost power and dove into the ground, killing him instantly.

Godfrey, on the other hand, apparently had it made. He had married, had two sons, became a successful businessman, and was elected to the Rhode Island State Senate. The man who President Roosevelt had called "Captain Courageous" had been awarded the *Croix de Guerre* with Star, the Distinguished Flying Cross with eight Oak Leaf Clusters, two Silver Stars, and a Purple Heart, and had destroyed 30.6 enemy aircraft. Unfortunately, John was stalked by a dreadful, incurable disease—ALS, or "Lou Gehrig Disease." He traveled extensively, visiting doctors and clinics in the States and abroad searching in vain for a cure. All efforts were unsuccessful, and he succumbed to the disease in June 1958, which accomplished what the Germans had never been able to do.

The two heroes who blazed their way through the *Luftwaffe's* best; whom Prime Minister Churchill had called "the Damon and Pythias" of the Twentieth Century; and whom Hap Arnold praised as the best combat team of the war each found death as non-combatants at the whim of enemies more relentless than any of the Nazis they had ever faced.

Major **JAMES A. GOODSON**

Major Goodson was a U.S. citizen, born in New York City 21 March 1921 of British parents. He was raised in Toronto, Canada, by his mother following his father's death. In 1939, upon graduation from high school in Toronto, he had no money but a great desire to meet relatives in England, so he decided to go to sea and shipout as a crew member. In hitchhiking toward the Coast he was sidetracked into the States, and his circuitous route involved a ride in a hearse which an automobile dealer had bought for the motor it contained. At night they stopped, and the dealer told Jim he could sleep in the back of the hearse if he wanted to. Being penniless he accepted the invitation. During the night two men and their girlfriends came along. The girls dared the men to open the door, which they did. The corpse suddenly came to life and sat up, causing them to retreat in haste. This demonstrates the inherent wit which Jim frequently found occasion to display.

Jim finally made it to the Coast and obtained a job aboard an ocean liner as a pantry boy. He made it to England and was able to visit his aunt and uncle in Sandwich, Kent, and then went on to France. He was in Paris when the Germans invaded Poland.

The French were unperturbed by this invasion, but Goodson found the British were quite concerned. He decided to return to Canada, booking passage on the *S.S. Athenia*, the last ship to leave Liverpool prior to war being declared. When off the Hebrides, the passenger ship was struck by a torpedo from a German U-Boat. Of the 112 killed 88 were women and children fleeing the growing conflagration in Europe. Goodson helped with the survivors and then had to swim to a lifeboat. They were subsequently rescued by a Norwegian tanker, which returned them to Galway, Ireland.

His anger was so aroused by the attack on this merchant ship that he immediately enlisted in the British Royal Air Force. He was sent to Canada to train. Back in Canada, the Royal Canadian Air Force introduced him to the rigors of flight training in Dunnville, Ontario. After having completed training in the RCAF on 12 May 1941 he was assigned, as a Sergeant Pilot, to the British Royal Air Force and sent to OTU (Overseas Training Unit), flying Hawker Hurricanes. On 6 June 1942 Jim joined his combat squadron, 416 Canadian, flying Spitfires. Jim saw plenty of action with the squadron, including covering the landing at Dieppe in August, a very bloody affair, flying dawn to dusk in support of Operation Jubilee.

On 24 August Jim was transferred to RAF No.133 Eagle Squadron, comprised mostly of American volunteers in the RAF and based at Debden, England. On 29 September the unit was accepted into the United States Army Air Force. Jim was in the 4th Fighter Group, 336th Squadron. As a Lieutenant in the newly formed Group he still flew Spitfires until January 1943, when U.S. planes became available. He, as well as the rest of the group, switched to P-47 Thunderbolts, a very different plane from the Spitfire, but nevertheless quite potent in its own right. They loved its firepower, ruggedness, range, and fast dive.

During a period of weather-related combat inactivity Jim took a short leave to London. He was a handsome, intelligent man with an impish grin and a trustworthy manner, which frequently favored the display of his hidden high-spirited wit. While having a drink with a new acquaintance—an officer from an Eastern country whose uniform hat was a maroon fez—Jim instigated an exchange of hats, his "Forty-mission Crush" for the maroon fez. Shortly thereafter he could be found touring his usual haunts wearing his U.S. uniform topped with his new fez. As might be expected, he soon encountered an MP who took exception to his strange attire and was intent on arresting him for being out of uniform. Jim, with his innocent smile and sincere demeanor, was successful in convincing the MP that he was on loan to the U.S. Air Corps, and being a Muslim, was allowed to wear his fez as a part of his religious beliefs. Upon return to Debden, still wearing the fez, his tale elicited round after rousing round of laughter at the Officer's Club bar.

With the advent of the P-47 there began a new chapter in the history of the Fourth Group. The increased range of the P-47 allowed victories to start accumulating. Colonel Don Blakeslee, the Group Commander, was not yet satisfied, and fought hard to get the P-51 for the Group and was finally successful. In February 1944 the Mustang was introduced into the conflict.

The Mustang had it all: the maneuverability of the Spit, firepower, and the range to go to Berlin and back. Goodson's first

victory, an Fw-190, on 23 June 1943, was followed by many more. He became proficient in knocking down *Luftwaffe* planes, and soon fifteen had found they could not outfight him.

In the meantime, he became known as the "King of the Strafers," wrapping up fifteen enemy aircraft destroyed on the ground for a total of 30 destroyed. The end of his combat with the Fourth was not the least bit unusual. Now a Major and CO of the 336th Squadron, he strafed Neu Brandenburg Airfield in Germany. A 20mm found its mark and he was badly wounded in his legs, but managed to crash land and hobble off into an adjacent wood.

He kept on the run for a week before being captured while trying to steal some food. He was questioned by the Gestapo and summarily thrown into solitary to be shot in the morning. Jim, who spoke German well, cleverly convinced the SS that he was too valuable to the Reich alive and was transferred to the *Luftwaffe's* jurisdiction. He was welcomed and duly interrogated by Hanns Scharff, the *Luftwaffe's* master interrogator. He was assigned to Stalag Luft III, and was transported by train through Berlin just in time to live through an Allied bombing. Arriving at Stalag Luft III, he was greeted by many of his friends who had preceded him.

During the winter of 1944/45 the Russians mounted an offensive, and as they approached the camp the Germans, in order to prevent their liberation, marched the prisoners south in a blizzard and the bitter cold of what became, for many, a death march. They finally were incarcerated in an abandoned prison camp at Nuremburg. Months later, it seemed likely that this camp would be liberated by Patton's Army as it penetrated German territory from the west. To avoid this possibility, the prisoners were again marched south toward Mooseburg, where they were held until finally liberated.

"Goody" had flown combat in Hurricanes, Spitfires, Thunderbolts, and Mustangs, and had 30 enemy planes to his credit. His decorations included the Distinguished Service Cross, the Silver Star, the Distinguished Flying Cross with eight Oak Leaf Clusters, the Air Medal with 20 Oak Leaf Clusters, the Distinguished Unit Citation, and the Purple Heart.

After the war he married Gwen, his English wartime sweetheart, and earned an MBA from Harvard University. Eventually he became head of two American companies in Europe and later a VP and Group Executive at IT&T. He retired to Duxbury, MA, where he enjoys the company of his son, James, and his three grandchildren.

I have known Goody for many years, and besides being an elegant gentleman, I can attest to his wisdom and great sense of humor. He has written an insightful book *Tumult in the Clouds*, which has prompted people to ask him "How did you remember all those details?" His typical tongue-in-cheek answer is "What I didn't remember, I made up." Now his most likely response to a common question is "Scotch and soda…double, no ice please."

Colonel **LEROY GOVER**

Although specific Royal Air Force records are lacking, Leroy's records indicate that he had shot down seven *Luftwaffe* planes, clearly indicating he was an Ace. His bio is therefore included in this book.

LeRoy Gover lived in San Carlos, California. He had the "bug" for flying and soloed a biplane on his sixteenth birthday. After graduating from high school he helped his father build homes, and learned the skills necessary to become a builder himself. In 1934 he bought a Piper Cub and spent two summers crop dusting in the Bakersfield area. He wanted to join the Air Corps but was not qualified, since he had no college education.

He heard of the Clayton Knight Committee, a group which was recruiting Americans to join the war effort and fly with the British and Canadian forces fighting the Germans. He applied for the RAF in May 1941 and was accepted. He trained at Bakersfield, CA, where he flew PT-17s and AT-6s. While in training there were inadequate housing facilities so the trainees lived in nearby houses and ate in a cafeteria in town.

Upon completion of his trainin there followed a wild boat ride across the stormy Atlantic to England. There he received additional training in an Operational Training Unit. He served in a British fighter squadron and then was transferred to No.133 American Eagle Squadron before joining the newly formed U.S. Army Air

Force 4th Fighter Group. The day before the transfer he knocked down a Fw-190 over Dieppe flying a Spitfire. He flew Spitfires in the RAF and then in the 4th Fighter Group, amassing 47 combat missions prior to the Group's switch to P-47s.

Lee had a tragic setback while on a duty to London to discuss the transfer from his British Squadron to the USAAF. His Squadron went on a mission to escort bombers with the weather badly overcast, and unpredicted winds blew the Squadron off course. They had eleven casualties due to running out of fuel and being shot down by flak, consequently wiping out his entire squadron.

The transfer was not without some trepidation. There were superior officers who wanted to split up the Eagle Squadrons' pilots among other U.S. groups to have the advantage of their combat backgrounds in training positions, but the Eagles would have no part of this. In addition, the British did not want to let them go. Rank considerations were also a problematic issue inasmuch as some were Sergeants and some were commissioned officers. There were not enough American planes to outfit the Group, and the British did not want to give up the Spitfires which they were flying. Finally, the problems were resolved to the satisfaction of most and the transfer became a reality, with the Group retaining the three squadrons and still flying Spitfires until sufficient American planes became available.

Upon transfer, since none of the Eagles had graduated from U.S. flight schools, American pilot's wings were issued en masse and the British wings were to be worn on the right chest. It seemed like the same outfit, more or less, still flying Spitfires being maintained by British crews. But the pilots were newly rich with the much more liberal pay scale of the U.S. forces and no one complained about that. Lee continued his luck (or skill) at winning heavily at dice, and he sent a large sum of money to his father with instructions to buy property for him.

Although the transfer to U.S. jurisdiction took place in September, it was not until February that the Group switched to American mess. This was a welcome change; no more "bubble and squeak." The Eagles began to receive P-47s, and immediately started becoming familiar with this chubby fighter. On 24 February Lee had to make a dead-stick landing which proved it was possible. 10 March saw the first operational flight in P-47s, and by the end of May Lee had flown 38 missions in the "Jugs."

On 9 July 1943 Lee was awarded the Silver Star, the first such award in the 4th Group. On 14 October he was promoted to Major, and on 12 December he was grounded for a mandatory leave having flown 234 hours on 159 combat missions in the P-47. Unfortunately, it took him until 12 March 1944 to get home due to the heavy load of returnees and limited shipping facilities.

On 30 May LeRoy was assigned to Page Field in Fort Myers, Florida, as Training Group Commander, where he served until the end of March 1945. He was then assigned to Luke Field in Phoenix, Arizona, where he flew two and four-engined bombers as Base Operations Officer at Kingman. In December 1945 he left the Service and went into the construction business. He soon bought a Great Lakes airplane.

The construction business was not all Lee had hoped for, and in 1947 he applied for a commission in the Army Air Force. On 19 June he was commissioned in the Regular Army and soon transferred as an officer to the Air Force. He was assigned as an instructor for the Air National Guard in Charlotte, North Carolina, where one of his duties was to fly 16 "Jugs" to California to fly in the making of the movie "Fighter Squadron."

His next assignment with the California Air National Guard gave him the opportunity to do something he had wanted to do for some time—fly a P-51. This was soon followed by subsequent assignments where he checked out in a jet (F-80), and later in an F-86, and he became a Squadron Commander.

In 1951 he was promoted to a Lieutenant Colonel. He was promoted to Colonel in 1961 and retired in May 1962. As a civilian he flew charter flights to Mexico and Canada, retiring in 1980 after accumulating 28,000 hours of flying time. Although RAF records of individual enemy aircraft kills are incomplete, Lee's records indicate he had four fighters shot down. He added three flying P-47s with the 4th Group.

He ended his career in combat as one of the most decorated fighter pilots in England. Upon retirement he had received 18 medals, including the Silver Star, the Distinguished Flying Cross with two Oak Leaf Clusters, the French *Croix de Guerre*, the British Distinguished Flying Cross, and membership in the American Caterpillar Club, a fraternity of those who had bailed out of an airplane and survived thanks to their silk parachutes.

Captain **HARRY N HAGAN**

Harry Hagan was from Yorkville, Ohio, and was assigned to the 4th Group, 336 Squadron on 1 June 1944 until 10 May 1945.

Returning from an uneventful mission 17 January 1945 flying a P-51 named "Duke," he lost power and bailed out, landing in a tree at Folkstone, U.K. At war's end he was sent to a Replacement Depot. He had five victories and was awarded a Purple Heart.

Captain **ROBERT D. HOBERT**

Robert Hobert was from Woodland, Washington. He was assigned to the 4th Fighter Group, 336 Squadron in May 1943 until April 1944.

Robert was on a strafing mission to Stendal Aerodrome 5 April 1944 led by Squadron Commander James Goodson. This highly successful mission destroyed approximately twenty-five German aircraft, including five destroyed by Don Gentile and six by Goodson. Hobert destroyed three Ju-88s, but reported his P-51 Mustang was hit by flak. Goodson did not observe much damage to Hobert's for base flying a P-51, but was downed in the North Sea for unknown reasons. He was rescued, but died in the hospital of exposure.

Robert Hobert had five victories to his credit and was awarded the Distinguished Flying Cross.

Colonel **JOSEPH H. JOINER**

Joseph Joiner grew up in Corpus Christi, Texas, where he dreamed of being a fighter pilot as he watched the Navy planes flying overhead from the Naval Air Station. When the war started, he applied to both the Navy and the Army pilot training programs. The Army accepted him first, and upon completion of the Aviation Cadet Program he was assigned to the 4th Fighter Group. He was really pleased to be assigned to the Fourth, having idolized the pilots who served with the Royal Air Force Eagle Squadrons.

His first squadron commander was Major James Goodson, who exemplified all the characteristics Joiner felt a fighter pilot should be: aggressive, daring, eager, talented, and a great leader. Johnny Godfrey, another of his icons, was also in his Squadron, and Joe considered him to be the most talented fighter pilot in his Squadron. Godfrey was a great natural fighter pilot and had the attribute of keen eyesight.

In time his flight commanders were shot down one by one, and he became a Flight Commander—prematurely he felt, since he had only 170 hours of combat and had graduated only nine months earlier from flying training.

On 11 September 1944, leading the last flight in the group on an escort mission to Halle, Germany, Joe spied a gaggle of 60-plus Me-109s flying directly over his Squadron heading in the opposite direction. He couldn't believe no one else had seen them. Inexperienced as he was, he did what, in retrospect, he considered to be the most stupid thing a flight leader could have done. He turned his flight of four 180 degrees to follow the 109s without notifying the Squadron Commander. His Wingman called to say they were friendlies, but Joiner answered they were 109s.

The Squadron leader, Major Fred Glover, hearing the transmissions, was calling for a fix, but at this time the Squadron was 25 miles away and could not possibly bring help to bear. Joe had no idea how to attack 60-plus 109s with his four ships but, as they climbed to the rear of the gaggle, he soon had his answer. Eight of the 109s turned to come at Joe's tail. His flight had to turn into the 109s, seven of whom split-S'd for the deck with Joe's three wingmen after them. Joe was left facing the leader alone. It was a long dogfight with maximum G maneuvers, but Joe finally got on the 109's tail and into firing position. He squeezed the trigger and nothing happened. He had neglected to arm his guns. As he found the problem and remedied it, the Hun had gotten onto his tail and the dogfight started all over again. More maximum Gs found Joe again in firing position. This time the guns fired and he got a couple of hits; the 109's canopy flew off and the pilot bailed out. In the meantime, Joe's #3 got one of the other 109s. Joiner regretted this ineptness, as he felt sure the Germans kept on their way to attack the bombers.

Joe went on to complete his tour and two additional 50-hour extensions. On 20 February 1945, on his third 50 hour extension, he flew his 84th and last combat mission. It was a fitting way to end his tour, as he shot down two Fw-190s. Colonel Stewart, the Group Commander, insisted that Joe take a 30 day leave to the States. While in Corpus Christi he heard the European War was ending, so he cut his leave short and returned to New York, hoping to rejoin the Fourth, which he felt would be heading to the Pacific, but for the Group and for him the war was over.

Later, Joe flew a tour in Vietnam in A-37s and OV-10s as a fifty-year-old pilot, but he felt the assignment did not compare with flying combat in WWII, which he considered to be the greatest experience of his life.

Joiner had many interesting observations about his combat career. As an example of these, he felt Colonel Blakeslee, Commander of the 4th, favored the RAF trained pilots over those trained in America, because he knew they were combat pilots by choice, having entered the fray prior to U.S. entry into the war. All his squadron commanders wore RAF wings. Joe felt Blakeslee was the greatest combat leader in the war. He was hard-drinking, tough, aggressive, and demanding. He had two objectives: to destroy the enemy, and to be the highest-scoring group in the war. He succeeded in both objectives. Blakeslee had no tolerance for mediocrity; he didn't like married pilots and considered them inferior to single pilots. He was a true warrior who loved combat and lived it to the maximum. He had more combat time than any other U.S. fighter pilot.

Joe felt that half of the pilots were flying to complete their tours and the other half were flying to destroy the enemy. He also felt that good athletes made the best combat fighter pilots. They needed split-second decision making ability, physical coordination, aggressiveness, and the ability to remain cool in stressful situations. He felt all combat he encountered ended up in one-on-one and, like many games, there is only one winner and one loser—in fighter combat the loser dies. Consequently, the tougher the game the harder you compete; easing up is not an option.

Joiner led 336 Squadron on 20 combat missions and the entire Group on two missions. Among his other notable accomplishments Joe flew a tour in Vietnam, a tour as Squadron Commander of F-102s in Greenland during the "Cold War," and he flew a P-51 on the first Air Force acrobatic team, "The Red Devils," in Las Vegas in 1948 and 1949.

After 30 years in the Air Force and 10,000 hours flying fighters he was amazed at what the Air Corps accomplished in WWII. Looking back, he finds it scary to reflect on how young and inexperienced we were.

Of course Joe is now retired. He plays handball every day and enjoys life to the fullest. He had 8.5 kills confirmed in the 4th, where he earned two Distinguished Flying Crosses, nine Air Medals, and a Unit Citation. After all of these experiences he feels he did nothing special. The readers will decide otherwise.

1st Lt. **GILBERT L. KESLER**

Gilbert enlisted from Washington, D.C. He served in the 4th Fighter Group, 336 Squadron from 7 September 1944 to 10 May 1945, at which time he was transferred. On 6 April he force landed a P-51 Northeast of Aachen, Germany, but was returned to base.

Lt. Kesler had five enemy aircraft destroyed to his credit. He lives in Littleton, Colo.

Major **WILLARD W. MILLIKAN**

Born 4 October 1918 in Hamburg, Iowa, Willard grew up and attended Peru State College. He wanted to join the Army Air Corps as an Aviation Cadet. In order to be accepted into the program he needed extensive dental work, which was very expensive. Finally accepted into the program, his worry over his debt distracted his attention to the point that his flying was unsatisfactory and he was washed out.

He went to Canada and joined the Royal Canadian Air Force, completed his training as a fighter pilot, and was sent to England. Upon U.S. entry into the war and the inception of the 4th Fighter Group, he transferred into the U.S. Army Air Corps and was assigned to the 336th Squadron.

During his time in England he married an English girl and they eventually had a baby daughter.

Millikan scored his first victory, an Fw-190. in September '43, and followed with three singles in the next six months. On 8 April 1944, during a scramble with a group of Me-109s near Ulzen he knocked down three to become an Ace. He later got another single, and then on 22 April he got four 109s near Kassel expending only 666 rounds of ammo.

On a mission 30 May "Millie," as he was known, took his squadron on a climb to rescue Deacon Hively, who was being chased by 30-plus Jerries. They dove for the deck closely followed by Millie's squadron. Down low, the flak gunners opened up and Millie's wingman, Sam Young, was hit. His plane reacted violently and its nose rammed Millie's plane, cutting it in half behind the pilot. With complete loss of controls the plane went into a spin, and as Millie released his seat belt he was violently thrown from the plane. As he plummeted downward he was unable to deploy his chute as the nose of his plane kept following him. The plane finally passed him in his descent and he belatedly opened his chute, landed, and was immediately captured by German soldiers. He spent the rest of the war as a POW.

Willard stayed in the Air Force until 1946, when he was discharged as a Major. He then served in the District of Columbia Air National Guard. As an employee of Goodyear, he set a West-East speed record in an F-86 flying from Los Angeles to New York in slightly over four hours. Eventually he retired from the ANG as a Brigadier General. He suffered a fatal heart attack in October 1979.

He had 13 confirmed victories and had earned the Distinguished Service Cross, the Silver Star, the Distinguished Flying Cross with four Oak Leaf Clusters, and the Air Medal with three Oak Leaf Clusters.

Maj. General **CARROLL W. McCOLPIN**

Major General Carroll McColpin was from Buffalo, New York. Born in 1914, he began flying at the age of 14. As a high school boy he built his own plane and taught himself to fly. He became aware that Britain was fighting fiercely to repel the Germans who were intent on conquering England in WWII, and he felt that the United States would sooner or later become involved in the war.

Rather than wait and take a chance on becoming a "ground soldier," he joined the Royal Air Force to be a pilot. He had pilot certification and over 475 hours of flight time. Like others with considerable flight time, he had no desire to spend the long tour in the mandatory U.S. Aviation Cadet Training Program when he was already an experienced aviator. He was sent to Dallas, Texas, for flight training in the Royal Canadian Air Force prior to being sent to England to an Operational Training Unit as a Pilot Officer. He eventually served in all three RAF Eagle Squadrons, becoming Commander of No.133 Squadron, and he soon had five aerial victories to his credit. As a Major he, with Chesley Peterson and Gus Daymond, became the first Eagle Squadron pilots to receive the British DFC on 4 October 1941.

McColpin, like many other fighter pilots, soon began to feel like he was invincible. Nevertheless, he was a good leader who inspired confidence in his men. He was proud of the fact that he never lost a man on a mission he led. He was older than most of the pilots and did not participate in the frequent social and drinking activities of those in the Group.

On 25 September 1942 he was ordered to London to discuss transferring to the U.S. Army Air Corps. He turned No.133 Squadron over to Flight Lieutenant Edward Brettell. On the 26th they were briefed to fly a more or less "routine" escort mission over France.

The weather briefing was quite inaccurate, and the twelve planes found themselves above a solid overcast with unusually strong winds from a direction totally opposite to the forecast. They did not pick up the bombers as scheduled and spent considerable

time orbiting waiting for them. Meantime, they were being blown way off course. They were low on fuel and, assuming they'd flown toward their base, they found a hole in the clouds and the Squadron dove through the hole, expecting to be near their landing strip. Instead, they were horrified to find themselves over Brest, one of the most heavily defended ports in France. Almost immediately six planes were shot down and the pilots became POWs. Four others were shot down with the pilots killed. One who had turned back early reached England and was seriously injured when he crash landed, and one parachuted over France. He was picked up by the French Underground and subsequently was returned to England. The entire Squadron was wiped out with its brand new Spitfires.

Carroll always set up his plane as he wanted it, and he wanted *his* plane whenever he was scheduled to fly. Of all the missions he flew, he most enjoyed what was called the "Rhubarb." It was fun flying a few feet off the ground shooting up trains, troops, tanks,

ships, or anything else of military value. He had an impressive career with 12 enemy aircraft destroyed. He had flown Hurricanes and Spitfires prior to being sent to the States on leave. He returned and served three tours in the European Theatre of Operations as Commanding Officer of the 407 Fighter-bomber Group and then the 404 Fighter Group. Later he was Director of Combat Operations for the 29th TAC. Still later he served as Commanding General of the 4th Air Force at Hamilton AFB, California. His awards include the Air Force Legion of Merit with two Oak Leaf Clusters, both the U.S. and the British Distinguished Flying Crosses, the Air Medal with six Oak Leaf Clusters, and both the French and the Belgian *Croix de Guerre*. He was decorated at Buckingham Palace by King George VI of England. He was one of the most decorated and admired fighter pilots in the war with 280 combat missions and 12 aerial victories.

Upon returning to the States in 1947 he commanded the 31st Fighter Group, entered the Armed Forces Staff College, and graduated in 1950. He was assigned to positions in the Air Defense Command and then entered the Air War College in 1954, graduating in 1955.

He subsequently served in many distinguished assignments, including Schweinfurt, Germany, and Newfoundland. He retired in 1968 as Commander of the 4th Air Force at Hamilton Air Force Base, California. Upon retirement, he went into the mortgage and investment banking business in Novato, California.

When McColpin entered the service he started in the Royal Canadian Air Force and was erroneously given the Canadian oath of allegiance. After having served in the United States Air Force until retirement as only one of two Eagle Squadron officers to be made General Officers in the Air Force, and receiving retirement pay for several years as a Major General, he discovered to his utter surprise he was not a U.S. citizen! He made this discovery when in the late '60s he applied for a passport for a trip and was denied! Wheels in Washington turned and soon he was awarded citizenship, and his passport application was of course approved.

McColpin died in November 2004.

Lt Colonel **ROBERT F. NELSON**

Robert Nelson was born in St. Louis, Missouri, and according to his account "then crawled to California two years later." His formal education ended at 16 when he began a photo engraving apprenticeship. He started flying in 1938 with Waco F-2s and was licensed in 1939. In 1940 he joined the Royal Canadian Air Force. Two years later, stuck as a staff pilot at an Operational Training Unit for observers, he had seen his classmates head out as bomber pilots, which he wished to avoid at all costs. His vision always had been to fly fighters.

One evening, as he was brooding in his corner chair in the Sergeant's Mess, he was called to the phone by his Flight Commander and informed he was to be flying "cine" gun detail at 7:30 PM. He didn't appreciate having his brooding and boozing evening interrupted for the sake of a few pictures, but he hit upon a plan to make the evening more interesting. He was aware that the CO's big cricket match would be in session and all the "knobs" (VIPs) would be there. This would be a good time to impress them with his positive attitude toward taking personal risk, in the hope that they might find him suitable to be a fighter pilot.

Arriving on the flight line at 7 PM, he carefully checked the Westland Lysander from nose to tail, looking for any possible flaw. Finding none, he climbed aboard and completed the cockpit routine, preparing to start the engine. He looked nothing like the pilots on the Royal Air Force posters. He was bareheaded, cotton wool stuck in his ears to protect them from the constant roar of the engine. A briar pipe protruded from the corner of his mouth, and for his scarf he wore a silk petticoat with "Pat" written across its bosom. He started the engine, tossed the "V" sign to his crew, and taxied out for takeoff.

After the final cockpit check at the end of the runway he headed into the wind and took off. He could see the crowd at the cricket match and thought to himself that he would show those knobs what made him a fighter pilot and that he didn't give a damn for nice safe soft jobs. Clear of the cricket field, he dove towards it to gain the necessary speed for a barrel roll. He brought up the nose and rolled. He thought maybe that wasn't low enough so he repeated the process—this in an aircraft in which aerobatics were prohibited. Upon landing he was immediately arrested, and soon became known as "Admiral Slow Roll" throughout the station.

As he tells it, during the next two days he and his guard managed to fill a saucer with cigarette butts before the CO released him without prejudice while he awaited Court Martial. During his wait he carried out normal flying assignments with those days counting against his sentence. He had accumulated ten days when the Court Martial took place. He was charged with "Slow rolling an aircraft in which aerobatics were prohibited, performing them under the minimum prescribed altitude, and endangering His Majesty's Westland Lysander and Flight Sergeant Pilot Nelson." The sentence was shocking, "... reduced to LAC (private first class) and fifty-six days of detention. Sorry old boy." Good behavior rewarded him with 18 days remission, and with his previous ten days of sentence served he had only 28 days of incarceration. Upon his release he became known as "Admiral Slow Roll, the Obedient."

During Nelson's incarceration he received notes of commendation about his flying ability and his positive attitude from two of his former COs, one of whom requested that he be assigned to his fighter squadron. He also received an offer of a pilot's job with the Westland Lysander Co. if he could arrange a discharge from the RCAF.

In November 1942 Nelson transferred to the newly formed U.S. Army Air Force, where he became a 1st Lt.

Fate turned against Nelson on 22 April '44. He and two other pilots were on a standby for giving blood transfusions to a needy patient, but the doctor released them, deciding to seek ground personnel for transfusions in case a mission might be scheduled. One was and Robert was chosen to go, flying as "Tail-end Charley." During the mission, near Kassel, Germany, his engine quit completely. He successfully bailed out, landing in a tree, and in an abortive attempt to evade capture he survived five days eating Buffalo Grass, which then became his nickname for the remainder of his year as a POW.

He was discharged in 1946 as a Captain. He had flown Spitfires, Thunderbolts, and Mustangs. He had six victories to his credit, and was awarded the Distinguished Flying Cross with two Oak Leaf Clusters, the Air Medal with three Oak Leaf Clusters, and the Caterpillar pin.

Following his discharge Bob attended college, did some reserve flying, tried crop dusting, a bit of parachute jumping (which at the age of 49 left him with some unfavorable impressions), and finally returned to photo engraving. Meanwhile, he managed to father five sons with the bonny Scotch lass Margery Forrest, MD, whom he married in 1943 as a perky young lady of 26. Margery was an exceptional woman. She had earned several gold medals for academic achievements, and at the age of 23 she had a degree of Bachelor of Medicine and a degree of Bachelor of Surgery from the University of Edinburgh.

Fast forward to 2008. Now retired as a Lt. Col., Bob is known as "Der Sveet Ol' Buzzard," and is busy etching beer cans preparatory to publishing a book, *The Art of Etching and Gravure with Beer Cans, Panty Hose, and Fish Hooks.* Following are pictures of some of his engravings with Air Force connotations. He, incidentally, cherishes a copy of U.S. Army General Orders sent to his wife, announcing the award of the Distinguished Flying Cross and the Air Medal to her much alive husband *posthumously*!

Lt. Colonel **WILLIAM J. O'DONNELL**

Col. O'Donnell, of Philadelphia, PA, joined the Army Air Corps in 1940. He, like most fighter pilots, had always had a yearning to fly. As a teenager he went through a Civilian Pilot Training program and obtained a private pilot's license. He then waited until he was old enough to become an Aviation Cadet and applied, with 13 others, for admittance to that program. He was the only one of the group to pass the physical exam and was enlisted in December 1940. Upon graduation at Craig Field, Selma, Alabama, he received his commission and his wings and became an instructor in single engine advanced training. In October 1944 he went overseas to England as a Captain and was assigned to the 4th Fighter Group, 335th Squadron. He flew a full tour with 63 combat missions and then transferred to 336 Squadron as Squadron Commander, the first of seven squadrons he would eventually command prior to his retirement. He had 5 enemy aircraft destroyed to his credit when the war ended.

In June 1945, at the end of the war in Europe, he was assigned to Shaw Air Force Base flying jets. When the Korean War started he was sent to Japan to the 8th Fighter Bomber Group, 36th Fighter Squadron. The current C.O. was a friend of Williams' and told him that he had one more mission to fly that day. He flew that mission and was killed. This found Willie as Squadron C.O. flying P-80s. To use the P-80s effectively they had to fly with oversized wing tanks which had no baffles. This frequently caused the wings to warp in the course of violent maneuvers. It soon became apparent that the P-80 was not a good plane for the close-in ground support work they were assigned to do in the hills and valleys. They had such a large turning radius that the pilots could easily lose sight of their target in the haze of battle.

O'Donnell got wind of a shipment of P-51s that was soon to arrive via an aircraft carrier. He made a deal and traded his P-80s for the P-51s. By a strange coincidence, in the shipment he found the P-51 that formerly had been assigned to him in the States. He immediately claimed it and named it "Mac's Revenge," after his friend who was killed on his last mission. The Group realized immediate success with the newly acquired P-51s. They carried

more ordnance; they had a shorter turning radius; and they carried enough fuel to remain over the target longer. They even found they had an advantage over the MiGs they encountered.

One encounter over Korea 200 miles from base had four Viet jets attacking them, firing their canons as they approached at 11,000 feet. The 51s turned into them firing their fifties as they went into a tight left turn. The jets could not turn with them and turned in a circle outside the 51s' circle. As a jet would go by a Mustang would pop out of the circle behind it and fire his fifties from behind the jet. By this means they heavily damaged three of the four jets and returned to base with no damage to themselves.

As the war proceeded they ended up flying out of an airstrip near Tague with armored tanks guarding the strip. An aggressive enemy was coming within mortar range of the base. One day they were so close William flew five missions never being out of sight of his crew-chief. The P-51s did an outstanding job against the North Korean advances, as they put extreme pressure on their supply lines by destroying all trains, trucks, and railroad bridges north of the front. After over 100 missions Willie was transferred to become Air Liaison Officer of the 3rd Army Division with an interesting job flying a Stinson L-5 spotter.

When he retired in 1961 he opened an insurance agency, which he operated until he retired again in 1985. In the meantime he married and had a daughter. Eventually this marriage was dissolved, and 10 years later he married again, this time to a woman who was a perfect match; a pilot, a nurse in WWII, and a good golfer. Unfortunately tragedy struck in 2001 when she was killed in an automobile accident.

Colonel O'Donnell was credited with five enemy aircraft destroyed in WWII and possibly a jet in the Korean War. He had earned the Distinguished Flying Cross with Oak Leaf Cluster, the Air Medal with 15 Oak Leaf Clusters, the Bronze Star with Oak Leaf Cluster, and the *Croix de Guerre* with Silver Star.

1st Lieutenant **DOUGLAS P. PEDERSON**

1st Lt. Douglas P. Pederson hailed from Long Beach, California. He was a copilot on a B-24. On one of his missions they had a serious accident and his crew was disbanded. At this point Doug applied for and received a transfer to become a fighter pilot. He was assigned to the 4th Fighter Group, 336 Squadron in November 1944, flying Mustangs. He claimed nine enemy aircraft destroyed—eight in one day, 16 April 1945—while strafing Praha/Kbely Aerodrome. This was a banner day for the Fourth with claims of 105 destroyed. The Group lost eight pilots and their planes; two were killed and six became POWs (all brought down by flak).

This seemingly banner day was not shared equally by the three Groups' squadrons involved. Becky Squadron, in which Pederson was flying, had 22 P-51s in the fray and destroyed 28 enemy aircraft. However, they lost seven P-51s, and they also lost the seven seasoned pilots flying them. Almost one-third of the Squadron was either killed or became POWs.

Lt. Pederson was flying #3 to the leader, Colonel Woods. On the first pass over the airfield Col. Woods, his #2, and his number #4 were shot down, and shortly thereafter four others were also lost, proving strafing could be a very dangerous occupation. Pederson's combat report states:

"While attacking Praha/Kbely Aerodrome, I was flying #3 to Colonel Woods. After the first pass, I never saw the men in my section again. They are all listed MIA. I made about 15 passes, destroying four enemy aircraft and receiving flak hits. I then moved north to Praha/Letnany and Praha/Cakovice Aerodromes and made six more passes, destroying four more huns. When my ammo was exhausted, I pulled up to 5000 feet and orbited the fields. I counted at least 60 fires burning. I was the last to leave."

The unusual aspect of this pilots' success is that he and four others (Capt. Robert Kanaga, 1st Lt. George Ridler, Capt. Gervais Ford, and 1st Lt. James Scanlon) had been assigned to the Group within a period of 8 months, all having served as B-24 pilots. Scanlon and Ford had each completed a tour of 35 missions, while Pederson, Ridler (a former BT-13 instructor), and Kanaga had limited B-24 time. Their similar backgrounds are best summed up by James Scanlons' account:

"James had trained his bomber crew at Tonopah, Nevada, and in July 1944, at the age of 19, flew them in a new B-24 from Hamilton Field, California to Nuts Corner, Ireland via Labrador and Iceland. He recalls, 'Existing in a bomber outfit is just that—EXISTING!' They were shot at on every mission and received flak damage 90% of the time. The food was bad, the huts were only one step above tents, the missions were long (many over 8 hours), all in close formation. Despite the specified maximum gross weight of 64,000 pounds, they were frequently loaded to 70,000 pounds. During James assignment with the 453rd Bomb Group, six planes crashed on takeoff due to ice or overload. To sum it up, there was no thrill to flying a bomber and it was extremely dangerous!"

When his 35 bomber missions were completed he applied for fighters and was accepted. After visiting four Fighter Groups he transferred to the Fourth, where he roomed with Bob Kanaga. His brother, Major Robert Scanlon, a B-24 pilot in the 15th AF, told him he was nuts and would probably get shot down. Ironically his brother, a Lt. Col. at age 26, was killed flying a Mustang on a ground attack mission north of the Pusan Perimeter, Korea, in September 1950.

Prior to starting the required 40 to 50 hours of P-51 time required to be eligible to go on operations Scanlon checked out in an AT-6. One brave instructor stuck with him for two hours and ten landings before clearing him to solo. He said, "If I wanted to kill myself it was OK with him, but *he* didn't intend to get killed by a *Bomber* pilot."

Sgts. Edlund and Paul Lucas showed him how to start the P-51 engine and gave him instructions; however, they neglected to tell him to burn the fuselage tank down to 25 gallons prior to pulling any serious "Gs." After trying all the usual flight maneuvers he decided to try some aerobatics. He nosed over, picked up speed to 320 MPH (the red line speed for a B-24), and eased up into a two or three "G" loop. During the process, somewhere near vertical the steed swapped ends and tumbled. Through no effort of his own he recovered and then returned to base to shoot landings.

Having been cleared to land, he set up his typical bomber landing routine and found himself approaching the runway about 800 feet higher than he should. The Tower told him to maintain heading and altitude while eight planes returning from a mission landed. For the next few minutes, each time he attempted to land he had to go around while more birds returning from combat came in to land. When he finally landed, the boys at dispersal thanked him for showing them where the field was. He had been flying his patterns just above where the haze combined with the setting sun had obscured the field to the incoming Group.

He flew many hours in P-51B models while building up his time. Occasionally he would get a "D" model, and he would ask for full drop tanks and go stooging alone over the Channel, looking for the flak batteries that hammered the B-24s as they entered the Continent. He said:

"The freedom and confidence I experienced after switching from a 64,000 pound bomber to a 10,000 pound fighter simply could not be imagined, felt, sensed, or experienced by anyone who has not made the switch."

After being declared "ops" ready he was able to get in a few licks at some seaplanes near Berlin, but was credited with only damaging three. However, he was glad to finally see the big picture, rather than the constant view of his leaders' wing as they flew close formation in B-24s. To see the bomber stream with fighters weaving all around was a picture he would never forget. He had a close call on a mission to Hamburg when his engine kept cutting out, but he managed to drag it back to base. The crew made a few mixture adjustments, possibly in the wrong direction, because on his next mission he crashed on take off due to extreme detonation.

After discharge Pederson, the only one of the B-24 pilots to become an "Ace," and Scanlon attended college together at the University of Southern California, until Scanlon was recalled to active duty in 1947. After 33 years in the military, with 12,000 hours of military and civilian flying, James considered himself a most fortunate AVIATOR! He had flown 45 different military airplanes and he had seen Berlin from the cockpit of a B-24 and from a Mustang 42 days later. He married and had eight children. He resides in Abilene, Texas.

Douglas Pederson dropped off the radar screen and no further information has been found.

Summary

Most people consider fighter pilots to be a special breed, as well they are. They are looked upon as being adventuresome, fearless, daring, and somewhat glamorous; much of which is true. Who else would knowingly volunteer for a job where you had a 40% chance of becoming a casualty, severely wounded, a POW, or killed? You daily faced the fact that of five of you having breakfast today, only three of you could have breakfast together at war's end. The Fourth Group facts are that during WWII there were 600-plus pilots assigned, of which 81, one out of every seven, became Aces, 264 became casualties, and 258 who did not become Aces finished their tours safely. It obviously was a dangerous profession! In spite of these facts, the Fourth destroyed 1016 *Luftwaffe* planes for a loss of 264 pilots. What is not so obvious from these observations is that the Fourth was always fighting over enemy territory, which contributed to their losses, as well as the fact that a very large percentage of their losses were the result of flak and not the result of aerial combat.

The pilots of the Fourth could compete in the air with the best the *Luftwaffe* could muster against them. Flak, however, was something else; it came at you silently, you could not see it and evade it, and its munitions could be quite deadly. Many of our planes succumbed to its irresistible force and, being over enemy territory, they as well as their pilots were permanently out of the combat.

It may seem strange that we are able to discover very little background information on several of our Aces concerning their lives before or after the war. From the time the group was preparing for D-Day until the end of the war, some records were not as complete as usual, and replacement pilots came into the group with little notice and left with little recognition. There were those who engaged in combat strafing aerodromes, becoming Aces and then being killed in action or becoming POWs, never returning to base and thus lost to the groups' records. Others were transferred to other groups or returned to the States, some never even having been photographed while in the Fourth. Their biographies are accordingly very short and represent all that was available in documentation.

Nose Art Gallery

The following nose art was created by Don Allen, a talented crew chief, during the height of WWII. His artwork was sought by members of 334 Squadron who were eager to display it on their planes. A few renditions are different but are attributed to the same pilot, who may have switched to a different plane during his tour of combat. These are reproductions, since the originals are long lost, but a few photos of the original work are included in the preceding text.

Turnip
Termite
©DON ALLEN '43
'94
LT. FRANK SPEER
QP-M P-51C 43-6957
334th Fighter Squadron
4th Fighter Group

FOURTH FIGHTER GROUP
DON ALLEN '45
'95
MAJOR FRED GLOVER
VF-B P51D 44-64153
336th Fighter Squadron
4th Fighter Group

Miss
DALLAS
TEXAS
©DON ALLEN 43/93
CAPT. VICTOR J. FRANCE
QP-K P51-B 43-6832
334th Fighter Squadron
4th Fighter Group

©DON ALLEN 43/93
LT. AUBREY STANHOPE
WD-O P-47 41-6233
335th Fighter Squadron
4th Fighter Group

LT. MARVIN ARTHUR
QP-U P-51D 44-73304
334th Fighter Squadron
4th Fighter Group
Blondie
© DON ALLEN '44 '94

© DON ALLEN '43 '94
LT. VINCENT 'BUD' CASTLE
QP-E P-47 42-7881
334th Fighter Squadron
4th Fighter Group
REAR FUSELAGE

LT. ANDREW STEPHENSON
VF-S P-47 41-6573
336th Fighter Squadron
4th Fighter Group
© DON ALLEN '98
Penguin Design by DON ALLEN
Painting on P-47 by Another

RIGHT COWLING
DON ALLEN 43/96
LT. KENDALL CARLSON
VF-E P47C 41-6575
336th Fighter Squadron
4th Fighter Group

OLD RED ASS
©DON ALLEN '43/95
LT. ROBERT BOOCK
QP-S P-47C 41-6405
334th Fighter Squadron
4th Fighter Group

ILL WIND?
©DON ALLEN 43/93
CAPT. NICHOLAS MEGURA
QP-P P-47
334th Fighter Squadron
4th Fighter Group

Miss Plainfield
©DON ALLEN 43/94
CAPT. STEVE PISANOS
QP-D P-47 42-7945
334th Fighter Squadron
4th Fighter Group

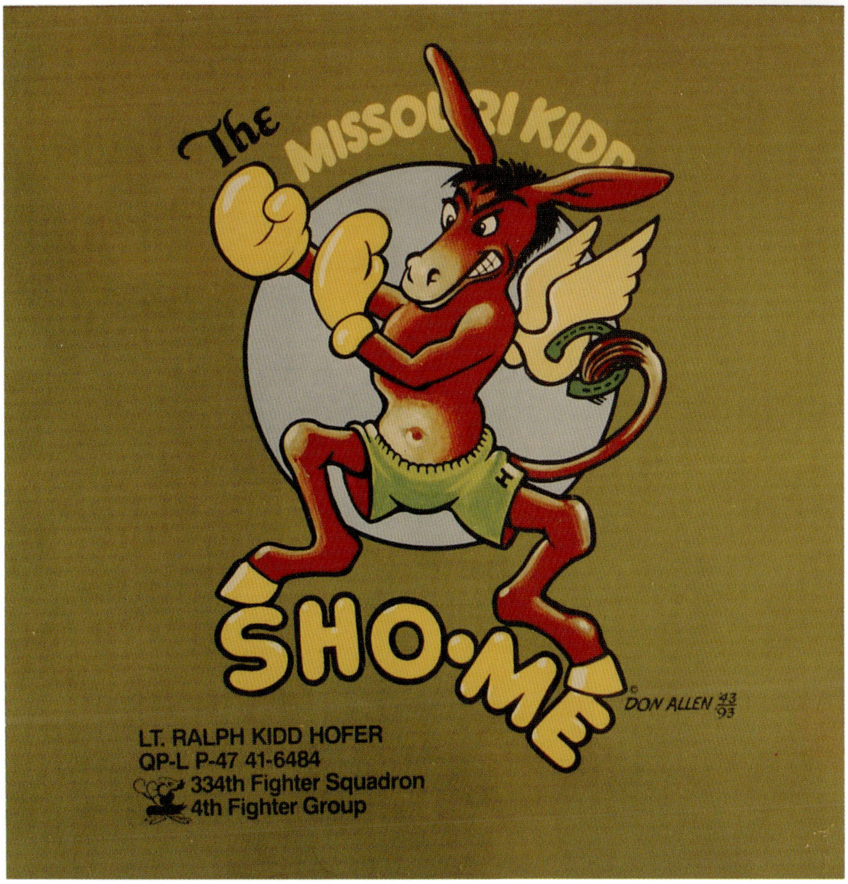
The MISSOURI KIDD
SHO-ME
©DON ALLEN 43/93
LT. RALPH KIDD HOFER
QP-L P-47 41-6484
334th Fighter Squadron
4th Fighter Group

Lilliput
1st LT. BREWSTER MORGAN
QP-U P-47 42-8644
334th Fighter Squadron
4th Fighter Group
© DON ALLEN

'04/DON ALLEN
© RAF Fighter Squadron Eagle
MAJOR ROY EVANS
WD-E P-47 42-74686
335th Fighter Squadron
4th Fighter Group

CALIFORNIA OR BUST
CALIFORNIA
SAN DIEGO (VIA BERLIN)
©DON ALLEN '43/93
CAPT. ARCHIE CHATTERLY
QP-G P-47 41-6358
334th Fighter Squadron
4th Fighter Group

©DON ALLEN '43/93
CAPT. WILLIAM O'REGAN
QP-X P-47 41-6392
334th Fighter Squadron
4th Fighter Group

The Count
©DON ALLEN 44/95
LT. RALPH BUCHANAN
QP-W P51D 44-72155
334th Fighter Squadron
4th Fighter Group

UNCLE DEN
DON ALLEN 43/94
LT. HERBERT BLANCHFIELD
QP-E P-47 41-6187
334th Fighter Squadron
4th Fighter Group

Sweet Arlene
© DON ALLEN 44/95
LT. A. REED BOWERS
QP-S P-51D 44-53223
334th Fighter Squadron
4th Fighter Group

QUACK
© DON ALLEN 43/94
CAPT. ROBERT PRISER
QP-L P-47 41-6187
334th Fighter Squadron
4th Fighter Group

MY Achin' Back
DON ALLEN 44/94
LT. PILOT UNKNOWN
QP-? P51D 43-731?5
334th Fighter Squadron
4th Fighter Group

©DON ALLEN 43/96
LT. MARK KOLTER
QP-Q P51B 43-71780
334th Fighter Squadron
4th Fighter Group

LT. EDWARD WOZNIAK
QP-T P-51D 44-63583
334th Fighter Squadron
4th Fighter Group

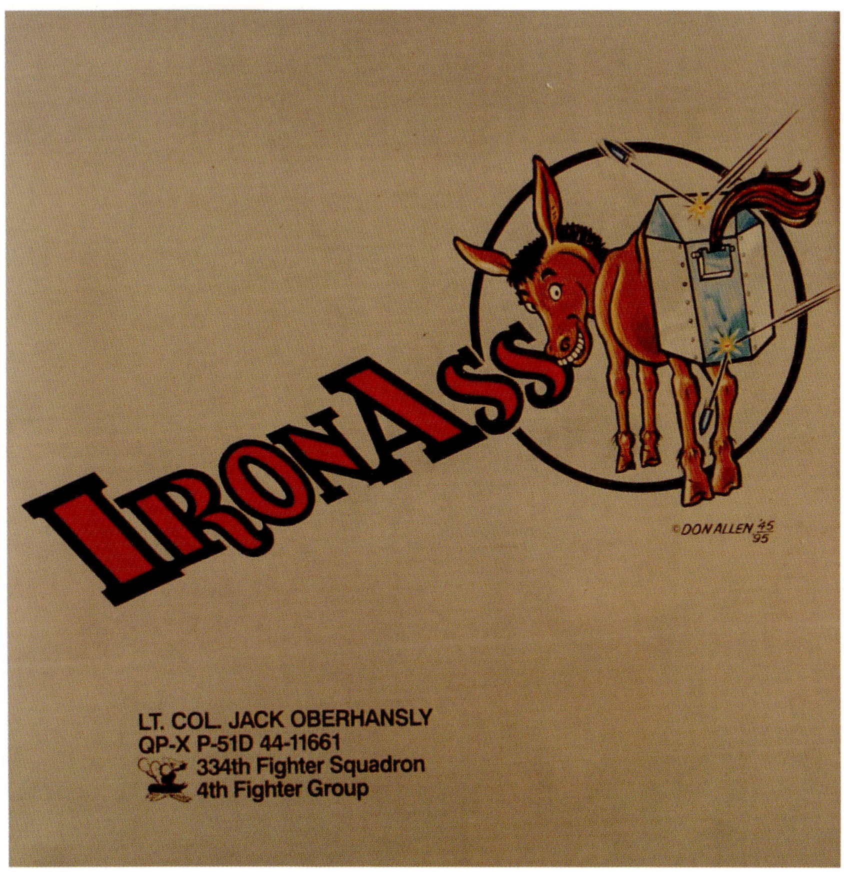

LT. COL. JACK OBERHANSLY
QP-X P-51D 44-11661
334th Fighter Squadron
4th Fighter Group

©DON ALLEN '43/'94
CAPT. WILLIAM B. SMITH
QP-Y P-47 41-6410
334th Fighter Squadron
4th Fighter Group
"Little Butch"

INDIANAPOLIS
INDIANA
©DON ALLEN '43/'95
CAPT. VERNON BOEHLE
QP-O P-47 41-6400
334th Fighter Squadron
4th Fighter Group

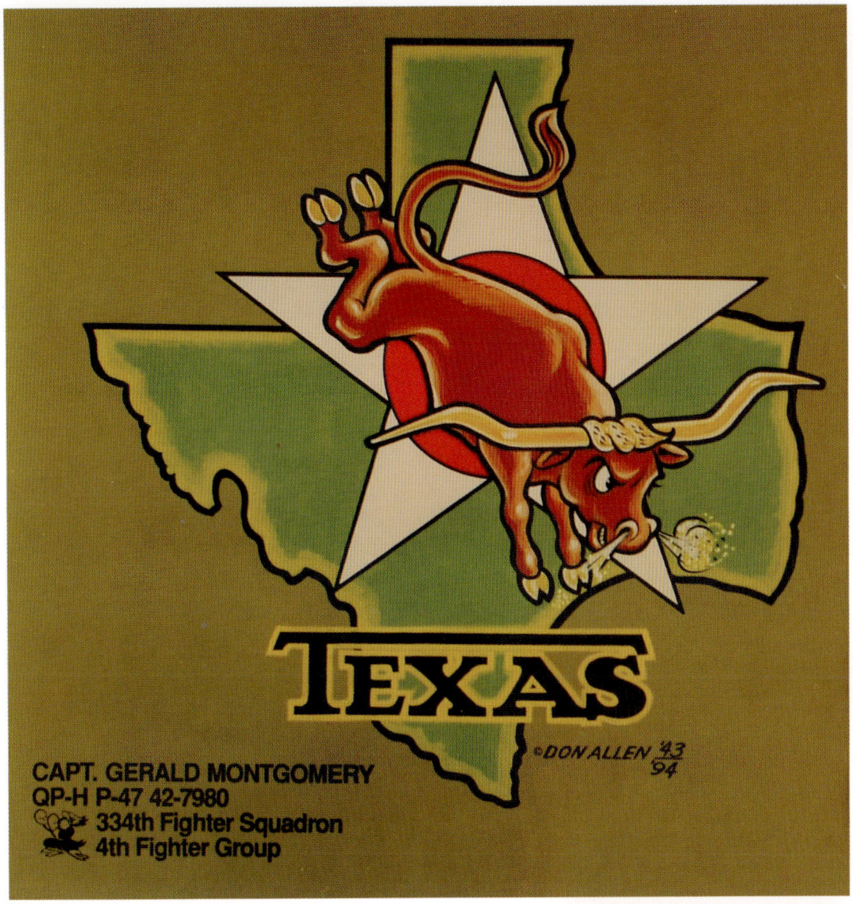
TEXAS
©DON ALLEN '43/'94
CAPT. GERALD MONTGOMERY
QP-H P-47 42-7980
334th Fighter Squadron
4th Fighter Group

WELA KAHAO!
©DON ALLEN '43/'93
CAPT. WALTER HOLLANDER
QP-B P-47 41-6538
334th Fighter Squadron
4th Fighter Group

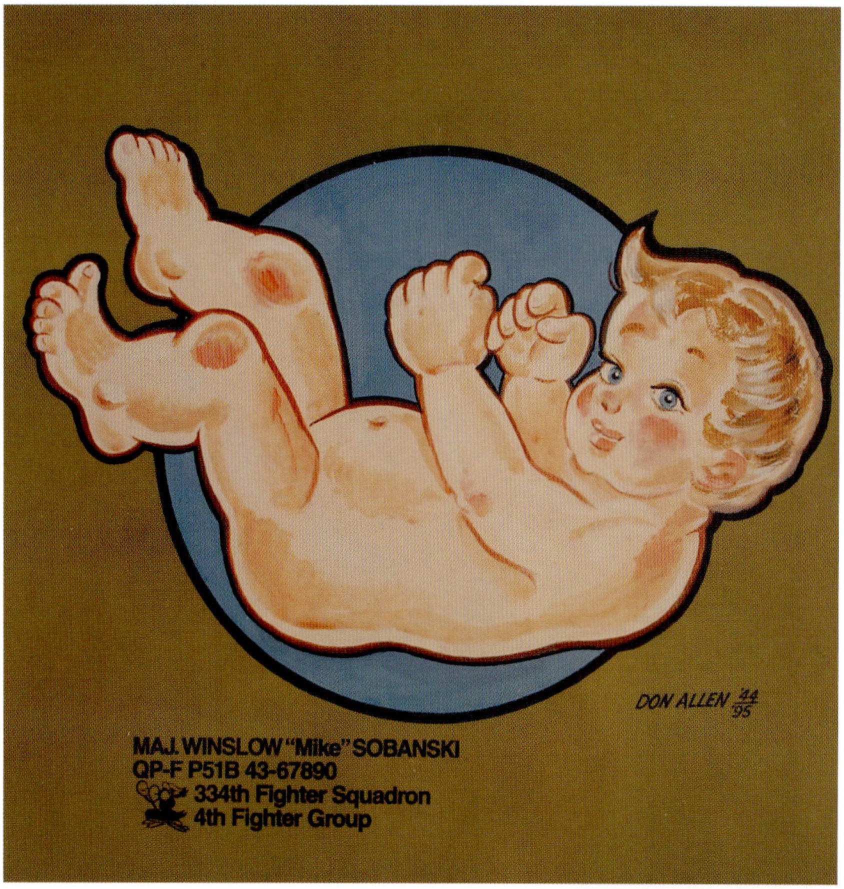
DON ALLEN 44/95
MAJ. WINSLOW "Mike" SOBANSKI
QP-F P51B 43-67890
334th Fighter Squadron
4th Fighter Group

CAPT. RICHARD McMINN
QP-M P47C 41-6204
334th Fighter Squadron
4th Fighter Group
©DON ALLEN 43/96

The "Mighty MITE"
DON ALLEN
LT. ROBERT S. SHERMAN
QP-D P51B 43-7002
334th Fighter Squadron
4th Fighter Group

Salem Representative
©DONALLEN 44/96
LT. RALPH KIDD HOFER
QP-L P-51B 42-106924
334th Fighter Squadron
4th Fighter Group

Old Witch
©DON ALLEN '45 98
LT. ROBERT VOYLES
QP-A P-51D 44-14292
334th Fighter Squadron
4th Fighter Group

Glossary

Buzz bomb – Germany's V-1 rocket powered, unmanned "flying bombs" launched from Europe, guided by radio to land somewhere in England when they ran out of fuel. Also known as "Doodlebugs" by the British.

Balbo (or Balboa – sometimes used with this spelling) – During the Chicago World's Fair in 1933, Italian General Italo Balbo led a flight of 22 Savoia Marchetti seaplanes from Italy to attend the celebration. Because of the great publicity surrounding that flight, during World War II any large swarm of aircraft was known informally as a "Balbo."

Bandit – Enemy aircraft.

Clobber – to do great harm, usually in reference to destroying another airplane. But the term was also used for everything from crap games to bad results in affairs of the heart.

Compressibility – the phenomenon associated with high speed in an aircraft. At a given speed, the air is no longer able to "move" out of the way of a wing leading edge, tail surface, etc., and it begins to compress, reaching higher pressure and sometimes causing the aircraft's controls to stiffen to the point of immovability.

Class A – formal Army uniform, consisting of dark green tunic and khaki trousers (the trousers had a notorious pinkish tinge, so Class As were also called "pinks and greens.")

Deflection (shooting) – angle for firing at another aircraft. Shooting from directly behind or head on is zero deflection; firing from a perpendicular position is 90-degree deflection, etc. Due to high relative speeds of two aircraft, the less deflection angle the easier the shot.

Dead stick – landing without power. Origin of the term is unclear. Could come from the lack of pressure on the control stick at slow speed; or stationary (dead) propeller.

Flak – Anti-aircraft fire of any kind. The word is an acronym for the German "flieger abwehr kanonen," the words mean literally "flier, against, gun."

French 40 and 8s – railroad boxcar designed to carry either 40 soldiers or eight horses.

Glycol – antifreeze coolant used in liquid cooled aircraft engines.

Ground loop – an accident on the ground involving losing control of the airplane and having it spin around, usually collapsing the landing gear.

Hun – derogatory word for German, based on historical reference to Attila's hordes.

Jerry – British term for Germans, most likely phonetic.

Kraut – derogatory word for German, based on their sauerkraut diet.

Kriegie – Allied shorthand for the German word *Kriegsgefanger*, meaning prisoner of war.

Rhubarb – a mission in which a small number of fighters penetrate enemy airspace at low altitude looking for ground targets of opportunity.

R/T – short for "radio-telephone"; a British term for an aircraft radio.

Split-S – aerial maneuver consisting of rolling upside down and diving for the ground, then pulling out to upright at high speed. Usually a defensive measure used when attacked.

Strafe/Strafing – Firing machine guns from an aircraft at ground targets. Derived from the German word for "punish."